Llewellyn's

2020

Witches'
Companion

A Guide to Contemporary Living

D0980650

Llewellyn Publications is a registered trademark of Llewellyn Worldwide Ltd.

Art Director: Lynne Menturweck
Cover art © Tim Foley
Cover designer: Lynne Menturweck
Designer: Joanna Willis

Interior illustrations:
Tim Foley: 9, 40, 67, 92, 126, 131, 140, 179, 198
Bri Hermanson: 33, 47, 57, 71, 221
Jennifer Hewitson: 105, 210, 231, 240
Rik Olson: 11, 79, 135, 149, 156
M. Kathryn Thompson: 21, 114, 163, 172, 183, 192

ISBN 978-0-7387-4952-5

You can order Llewellyn annuals and books from *New Worlds*, Llewellyn's magazine catalog. To request a free copy of the catalog, call toll-free 1-877-NEW-WRLD or visit our website at www.llewellyn.com.

Llewellyn Publications
A Division of Llewellyn Worldwide Ltd.
2143 Wooddale Drive
Woodbury, MN 55125-2989
www.llewellyn.com

Printed in the United States of America

Contents

Community Forum

Provocative Opinions on Contemporary Topics

Magical Self-Care

Nurture Your Body, Mind & Spirit

Witchy Living

Day-by-Day Witchcraft

Witchcraft Essentials

Practices, Rituals & Spells

The Lunar Calendar

September 2019 to December 2020

Community Forum

PROVOCATIVE OPINIONS ON
CONTEMPORARY TOPICS

Coven or Cult? How to Tell If Your Group Has Crossed the Line into Dangerous Territory

Storm Faerywolf

While the word *cult* technically refers to any small group with a common set of beliefs (*Star Trek* and *Doctor Who* each have a "cult following," for example), in popular parlance it takes on a much more sinister connotation, offering hints of coercion, control, harassment, abuse, and sometimes even murder.

A cult, in the negative sense, doesn't always start out that way. Some cults begin as positive religious groups but somewhere along the way become corrupted, perhaps slowly exerting more pressure on their members until they eventually find themselves brainwashed. This slow progression can be a major contributing factor in the subjugation of a group's

members. If the negative behaviors are gradual, members are less likely to rebel or even notice them until the group has crossed over from legitimate congregation to actual cult. And even then, they might not.

While many people are familiar with the tragic story of Jonestown (where, in November 1978, 918 people lost their lives in a mass homicide-suicide at the command of the group's leader, Jim Jones), more might be surprised to know that before he led a suicide cult, Jones preached racial equality and other progressive philosophies to his congregation. If there is such a thing as an expected scenario that gives birth to a dangerous cult, this isn't it.

A commonality in cults is the level of control that leadership has over its members. This is easily seen in organized religions in which a central body of authority dictates to the masses what is to be believed or practiced. But this same corrosive mentality can infect non- or lesser-organized religions as well.

A powerful feature of the Witch's coven is the concept of the group mind. This is the collective spirit that forms when a group regularly does magic together. This spirit assists the group, offering guidance, inspiration, protection, and power. It is nourished by the consciousness of the group's members and can be seen as a sort of tribal totem or deity.

But what happens when one or more of the group's members have duplicitous or nefarious intentions, dangerous addictions, or even severe mental illness? The answer is that this group mind is adversely affected, perhaps even taking on those addictions or illnesses. Members may become increasingly paranoid that others are out to destroy them. Small personal slights are magnified into religious-level crusades. Differences in theology or opinion are used to justify personal attacks or vindictive behavior. In effect, the coven becomes "cursed," a victim of its own broken Witches.

Members of these damaged covens are often instructed not to socialize with others outside the group or lineage or are told to

Members of these damaged covens are often instructed not to socialize with others outside the group or lineage or are told to avoid certain individuals. Information may be restricted, with leaders oftentimes telling congregants that certain books or materials are forbidden, especially those that challenge the teachings or politics of the leadership.

avoid certain individuals. Information may be restricted, with leaders oftentimes telling congregants that certain books or materials are forbidden, especially those that challenge the teachings or politics of the leadership.

Sadly, these groups persist. They will tell themselves (and anyone else who will listen) that they are the only "true" version of the Craft or their tradition as they quietly (or not so quietly) labor to undermine the work of others. And they have been given a near-perfect weapon to do so: the internet.

I have some personal experience with this. Being a public teacher of the Craft has had its ups and downs. Since Faery tradition has no central authority, this has resulted in individual covens and lineages having their own values and even practices. While this is a healthy thing for the most part, it has also resulted in environments being created in which egos are given room to expand largely unchecked. If people isolate themselves in an echo chamber of matching opinions and views, then they quickly lose touch and begin to believe the otherwise unbelievable. This is one of the most dangerous aspects of the cult mentality; for the most part, members will not even consider that they are "in a cult," because that was likely not their intention or experience when joining. It is only when confronted head-on that the glamor is exposed, the illusion is dispelled, and the sickening reality becomes devastatingly clear.

That glamor was dispelled for me in 2003. Having spoken publicly about my personal experiences with a sexual predator in our tradition, an elder priest of Faery, I was shocked to encounter not only the many others who had been similarly mistreated but also the resistance that many had to hearing the truth. Almost immediately, the charges of "oathbreaker" began to surface, for I had dared to speak out against a beloved elder. Now I was fair game for attack, verbally and magically. This was the beginning of what would later morph into targeted harassment.

In the midst of this, my husband described the situation to a mundane coworker, who replied, "Dude, you're in a cult!" As he tells it, suddenly everything clicked into place for him. When my husband relayed the story to me, I likewise had the same epiphany. I hadn't originally joined a cult, but over time, through casual and sustained interaction with the more conservative members outside of my own group, I had unconsciously "bought in" to a cult mentality. But now I saw it clearly.

While most of the relationships I have with other initiates of our tradition are positive and meaningful, because of my status as a public teacher, some of the more "conservative" (and from where I'm standing, fundamentalist) members of our tradition are uncomfortable with me at best and downright hostile at worst. I have been the target of online harassment from a small group for years. They actively recruit others, put up attack websites, fabricate scandalous stories, contact my students to privately "warn" them, negatively comment whenever my name appears in a blog, etc. At first this was painful and confusing, but now I just find it sad that they have nothing else in their lives of value than to obsess over what I am doing. I got out of the cult mindset a long time ago. They, sadly, are still very much in it.

If anyone can read a book and start a coven, it means that students need to be discerning and take charge of their own education. Once a seeker has read a few books on modern Witchcraft, they should be prepared to recognize some of the warning signs. But since so many of these signs are easy to miss, here is a quick list of both red and green flags to consider when determining if your group has gone from coven to cult.

Red Flag: Restricting Information

If participation in the group comes with an insistence on avoiding certain books, ideas, people, etc., then this is a big red flag. A legitimate teacher will not fear knowledge but will use even bad information as a means to further illustrate their teaching. I know of multiple instances in which a teacher has forbidden a student from reading certain books or visiting certain websites, invariably because the information there is in conflict with the cult's point of view. A healthy teacher or religion will not tell you who your friends should be.

Red Flag: Persecution Complex

Oftentimes a cult thrives on identifying an "enemy," upon which they will project any number of nasty intentions. If one of the first things you hear from a group of people is about who they hate, maybe that should be an indicator of the type of people they are and the biases they are harboring.

Red Flag: Isolation

Cults will often form into insular units that have little or no contact with the outside world, or when they do interact, it's usually only to act as a mouthpiece for the cult. Members are encouraged (and, in some cases, ordered) to disassociate from "outsiders," especially those who have expressed criticism of the cult's beliefs or practices. This is often achieved through giving and withholding attention and favor within the group, and may not be a formal command but instead a sort of "custom." ("The leader doesn't like X, so to get on their good side, I don't like X either.") Once members are immersed in an environment where they mentally live inside the cult more than they do outside it, they become prone to seeing exclusively through the cult's mental lens, making their further subjugation more likely.

Red Flag: Sexual Currency

The modern history of Paganism is littered with stories of those who have been sexually abused or otherwise coerced in connection with learning the Craft. Because Witchcraft is deeply rooted in sexuality and primal power, sex is often a tool used by unscrupulous groups to ensure loyalty and maintain control. Some may require a student to submit sexually to their teacher, sometimes under the pretense of practicing a supposed "older model." This model, in which teacher and apprentice are somehow equals (giving said teacher the freedom to indiscriminately bed their students without repercussion), is based largely on fantasy and conveniently disregards all evidence that these types of relationships are often harmful. There's good reason why professional institutions generally forbid them. Argue that said teacher and apprentice are really equals, and what is revealed is a flimsy excuse for maintaining ethical blinders. If a group or leader requires members to have sex with someone, it is a form of cultic rape. Even if sex is not required but is used as a means to advance those who engage in it beyond those who don't, this is still an egregious abuse of spiritual authority. When one party holds power over another, consent cannot be fully given, even if those in the "lesser" position feel they are capable. Legitimate teachers should take care to ensure that they do not practice or condone such corrosive behavior.

While there is and should continue to be a place within the Craft to work sexually with each other, these workings should be done between equals and not while one possesses authority over another. One consideration is when preexisting lovers wish to share the Craft's mysteries. One still might be instructing the other, but their connection is not based on a model of imbalanced power.

Green Flag: Transparency

A healthy coven will operate in the open, meaning that members will not be shielded from the leadership's process of decision making and operations. If there are class fees or other obligations for membership, then those stipulations and any additional policies will be clearly stated up front. And the human flaws of the group's leadership will not be covered up. There may be secrets that are kept from even most members, depending on one's rank within the group (as with many degree systems or initiatory lineages of the Craft), but those secrets will be along the lines of specific ritual actions or liturgical symbolism, and certainly not the activities or behavior of the leadership.

Green Flag: Inclusivity

A healthy group will encourage members to maintain their friendships and interests outside of the religion. Healthy group leadership is not threatened by outside voices, even those that may be critical of their philosophies or beliefs. This also extends to former members, even disgruntled ones. A healthy leader or group will not spend time vilifying former members or forbidding current members from associating with them. Additionally, sources of information will not be forbidden or shunned; a free exchange of ideas will be encouraged.

· · · · · · · · · · · ·

If you have experienced one of the Red Flag items listed here, then your group might be in the early stages of becoming a cult. If you have experienced two Red Flag items, then your group appears to be on its way to culthood and you may need to leave or confront the leadership, if it is safe to do so. Three or more experiences with Red Flag items make a strong case for culthood. May your eyes be open, and may your path always be one you walk in freedom.

Resources

Bonewits, Isaac. "The Advanced Bonewits' Cult Danger Evaluation Frame." http://www.neopagan.net/ABCDEF.html.

Cult Education Institute. "Warning Signs." https://culteducation.com /warningsigns.html.

Storm Faerywolf *is a professional author, experienced teacher, visionary poet, and practicing warlock. He has been initiated into various streams of Witchcraft, most notably the Faery tradition, where he holds the Black Wand of a Master. He is the founder of his own lineage of the tradition, BlueRose, and the author of* Betwixt & Between *and* Forbidden Mysteries of Faery Witchcraft. *For more, visit faerywolf.com.*

A Higher Spirituality: Cannabis

Kerri Connor

Less than a hundred years ago, right here in the good ol' United States of America, people were brainwashed into believing cannabis caused its users to go temporarily insane. They were taught that this plant would create a blood lust and invoke its users to commit suicide, partake in violent crimes, give them superhuman strength, or commit murder.

Today we know that is nothing but hogwash.

Stepping into the Light

At this writing, many states have laws allowing for the medical use of cannabis, with more joining in all the time despite the current federal ban. (With any luck, by the time this article is published, cannabis will be federally recognized as the miracle plant it is, declassified as a schedule 1 drug, and made legal for *all* uses nationwide.) Several states have gone one step further and legalized recreational use as well.

But while the debate over medical and recreational use is ongoing, you seldom hear about spiritual use. Now, yes, I suppose technically you could argue that spiritual use would go under recreational use, but for people who use alternative healing methods to begin with, their spirituality is often strongly connected to the medical/physical side of life. Besides, there is truly a huge difference between getting high for fun and getting high for spiritual purposes. The spiritual aspect does not get brought into the discussion, but it's about time it did.

Even in the pagan community there is much debate about whether cannabis is useful or harmful. I believe this subject is even more divisive in the US because many of us grew up in an environment where cannabis was demonized in all forms on a national level. But for generation after generation, cannabis has been used all over the world in a variety of religions and spiritual practices. Because of its healing and entheogenic abilities, it has been a component of spirituality for thousands of years.

Overcoming Skepticism

The most common reason given by pagans not to use cannabis is the belief that it clouds your mind while putting you in an altered state. This argument says the mind should be clean, clear, and sober.

The first part of this—that cannabis clouds your mind—simply is not true. Can some strains of cannabis make you feel cloudy? Can some doses of cannabis make you feel disoriented? Yes to both! But that does not mean *all* strains or *all* doses do the same thing! What

it does mean is that each one of us is different and requires different strains and doses to hit the peak spiritual experience. When you find a good strain and dosage for you, you will find that your brain is just the opposite of cloudy! Cannabis at a peak experience opens your awareness exponentially. It multiplies the intensity and power of all your senses. Your focus is extremely sharpened.

When you find a good strain and dosage for you, you will find that your brain is just the opposite of cloudy! Cannabis at a peak experience opens your awareness exponentially.

The second half of this argument—that cannabis puts you in an altered state—is true. That is precisely why it is so beneficial for people spiritually. Meditation, trance, shamanic journeys, drawing down the moon—all of these are altered states. Cannabis helps to bring down the barriers in the mind that prevent the user from accessing these altered states. It also creates a deeper, more intimate connection with spirit/deity and provides an alarm clock that will allow you to naturally and comfortably release or end your session when your high fades away.

The greatest benefit of using cannabis in a spiritual practice is what happens when these two aspects join together. While in the altered state that cannabis provides, with this incredibly deep connection to spirit, you are still fully aware. This is the exact state of mind and spirit you want to achieve. This is the peak experience millions have used spiritually over centuries. From Hindus, to Zoroastrians, to Sufis, to Taoists, to Buddhist monks, to Zulu warriors, to Pygmie tribes of Africa, to the Rastafarians of Jamaica—all these people and more have used cannabis in their spiritual practices. When it comes right down to it, it seems silly for non-users to believe they have more knowledge about the plant and its uses than those whose religions have used it for millennia.

Now that more states are making cannabis legal, whether through medical or recreational use, more people are learning of the benefits of working with cannabis in a spiritual sense as well. Whether they come across the spiritual aspect by mistake or by design, it is heartening to see more people open to the spiritual possibilities of cannabis.

For those who have a difficult time getting out of their own mind to make practices like meditation or trancework even possible, cannabis is a brilliant option. In fact, as an earth-loving, tree-hugging, hippie kind of pagan, I must believe the Goddess sent us cannabis partly because it works as a communication system. It gives us access to spirit, our higher selves, and deity. What more could we ask for? If this plant is so bad, then why is it so perfect in so many ways? It heals many ailments and helps many people make a spiritual connection, including those who haven't been able to do so on their own. Our society is in dire need of the healing and spiritual capabilities of cannabis.

Some cultures believe that the cannabis plant is an incarnation of the Goddess herself, as it is the female plant that flowers and provides us with the power to easily connect with her spiritually. I find this belief to be both fitting and soothing. What could be more perfect than the Goddess offering a piece of herself to aid in connecting spiritually with her?

Because You're Worth It

Unfortunately, there are pagans who believe that if someone cannot make that spiritual connection on their own, then they are simply not ready to make that connection. I have to call hogwash on that too. That is an extreme, elitist view that basically says everyone who ever used cannabis spiritually before wasn't ready to make a spiritual connection. All those shamans, all those monks, all those *everybody*; people who were born and raised into those roles their entire lives. It's insulting. It's also insulting because it implies that the person who cannot make that connection on their own doesn't deserve to.

We all have different strengths and weaknesses and different gifts. What I am good at, you might be awful at. Where I'm terrible, you may excel. This is no different. Just because someone may have a difficult time making a spiritual connection doesn't mean they don't deserve the opportunity to make one. It also doesn't mean they shouldn't be able to use tools available to them to make that connection. Cannabis is simply a tool to help—a very effective tool.

Ostracizers Need Not Apply

Finally, do we really want to be telling other pagans that they shouldn't be able to connect with their own deities in their own way? Do we really want to tell them that the only way to "earn" that spiritual connection is through a practice that might not ever work fully for them? Especially if there is an option that does work for them and does give them the opportunity to connect with deity on a one-on-one basis?

Let's also take a moment to recall how the Catholic Church decided that people needed an intermediary between them and God. They had to have saints and priests be their go-betweens, as it was considered heretical to talk to God on their own. We, as pagans, have a tool that has been given to us to help us connect spiritually with deity. If it wasn't supposed to work that way, then nature made a terrible mistake. See how ridiculous that sounds?

There are people who will not agree with my point of view and will believe, no matter what, that cannabis is an awful, hard-core drug. But there are some out there who have either experimented with it or thought about it, or are a little on the fence and want to know more but are too afraid to ask. If you are one of these people, this article is for you.

Get High with a Little Help from Your Friends

The most important aspect of using cannabis spiritually is finding precisely what works for you. If you are new and afraid to experiment but want to try, my best piece of advice to you is to find a partner. This can be anyone who is open to the idea of you experimenting with cannabis and is someone you trust. It can be a spouse, a friend, or a family member. It can be an experienced cannabis user, someone who is curious and open to experimenting, or someone who has no desire to use but isn't bothered by the fact that you do. This person is there to reassure and protect you if necessary and in case you do have foggy moments. While you experiment, your partner does not. Take turns and return the favor. The partner will serve as a guide (they can walk you through guided meditations), a protector, and a recorder of tales.

Research, Record, Relax

There are decisions you will need to make about what delivery system you use, but that is completely up to you. What you do need to make sure you know is what you are using. If you are able to use a product that gives you the strain and THC information, that's great! Be sure to keep a journal to record this information. You will also want to record things such as the delivery system you use, how much you use, and for what duration. Having a partner makes recording all this information easy, as that is their job.

If you don't have a lot of information about what you are using, you should at least know if it is a sativa or indica strain. If you don't know this, your experimentation may not go as planned. Sativa strains tend to be uplifting and energetic, while indicas are more suitable generally for meditation and trance work due to their calming and relaxing effects. There are also hybrids that are a combination of the two. While indicas are calming, some may also cause paranoia at certain doses. This is also where your partner comes in. If paranoia or anxiety does set in, your partner is right there to get you through it. Just about everyone who has ever used cannabis has experienced both. Try to remind yourself that it is temporary and will pass.

The first important step is to know what you are consuming, and the second is to go slow. Cannabis affects different people differently, and different strains affect different people differently as well! Whatever you are using, start small and slow. Some people get high very quickly, others more slowly. The method of delivery affects the speed of onset too. Edibles take the longest to take effect, though they have a longer staying power. Less can be more when using cannabis. Start with a small dose, then twenty minutes later, add another if you need to. People who haven't used or who seldom use will have a lower tolerance level. What works well for you might not work well for your partner.

The first important step is to know what you are consuming, and the second is to go slow. Cannabis affects different people differently.

It takes time, patience, and practice to find what you are looking for and to learn how to put yourself into the state you want to be in. For gentle meditation, you may not need or want much. You can go with what relaxes you and feels comfortable for you. But for shamanic journeys, trance work, and especially drawing down the moon or other deity communication, you want to hit that peak spiritual experience. You will learn over time what works best for you and how much you need to achieve and maintain the experience you want.

The first few times that you hit the peak experience, it may sneak up on you. As you experiment, focus your attention on how you feel and communicate that to your partner to record. Sometimes it may feel like you dropped right on top of the peak, while other times you may feel yourself climbing into the high. Again, this may depend on what and how much you consume.

How will you know when you hit the peak experience? You will know. You will know because your body, mind, and soul will tell you so. You will realize that your senses are all far more powerful than you ever remember them being. Playing soothing music while you experiment not only will help you relax but will enhance the experience by giving your hearing something to focus on. You will not be giggly or hungry or paranoid. That's not to say those things couldn't come about at a different point in your session, but they will not be present during a peak experience. You will feel uninhibited (another reason your partner needs to be trustworthy). When you feel it, describe it to your partner so they can record it (along with the time) for you. What you may feel is a peak experience in one session may pale in comparison to a peak experience down the road. Documentation helps you learn from your experience even after it's over.

A typical journal entry could be something like this:

Skywalker [this is the strain]: *total THC 27%*

Session began at 7:15.

Smoked, took 4 hits in 10 minutes.

Lightheaded at first. Felt like there were pins and needles—electricity flowing through body.

7:32 Music became very clear-sounding, more beautiful than remembered.

Described as floating. Reported feelings of peace and contentment.

7:58 Munchies set in.

Learning to use cannabis spiritually is very similar to using it medically or just for a fun high: you have to know what it takes to get you to the optimum level for your needs. This takes time and a lot of trial and error. You may have some bad experiences with paranoia or anxiety, or you might not have any at all. Remember that any negative feelings will fade, and your partner is there with you.

The power and intensity cannabis brings—not only to deep trance-like workings but to everyday meditations as well—is a whole new element you can bring to your own spiritual practice. When you feel truly at one with the universe is when you learn to help and heal the universe as well as yourself.

Working with someone else in this manner is very intimate, which is another reason you need your partner to be someone you trust. The two of you can work together at the beginning of this journey until you feel comfortable and experienced enough to go it alone. Then make yourself available to mentor and pass on what you learn to others and help them feel safe on their own enlightened spiritual journey with cannabis.

Kerri Connor has been practicing her craft for over thirty years and runs an eclectic family group called the Gathering Grove. She is a frequent contributor to the Llewellyn annuals and the author of Spells for Tough Times as well as a guide to spiritual growth through cannabis to be published by Llewellyn in 2020. Kerri resides in northern Illinois.

Not a Real Witch: Authenticity and Imposter Syndrome

Thorn Mooney

I discovered Wicca when I was about fourteen. Like many young people who come to the Craft, I didn't feel like I quite fit in. I was obsessed with mythology and ghost stories, I was much more comfortable out in the woods by myself than with other people, and, though I wouldn't have admitted it in front of my peers, I never quite stopped believing in magic. Introverted and weird, I was bullied in school. So imagine—as I'm sure many of you can—what a profound relief it was to discover witchcraft! Reading my first books and casting my first circles felt, as it does for many, like coming home. Suddenly my life made sense, and the world felt more exciting. And I had a place in it! A community of people like me, even! I couldn't wait to find them.

What a blow it was to discover that this community wasn't always as welcoming as I'd expected it to be. As a young teenager, enthusiastically clutching fresh copies of Scott Cunningham and Silver RavenWolf, I was shocked to be called a "fluffy bunny" and told that I wasn't a "real" witch because I was too young and too inexperienced. Undeterred, I kept learning and practicing. Then I went back out into the Pagan world, but the criticism hadn't gone anywhere. Being older, I didn't get called as many names, but I was still told I wasn't a real witch, this time because I wasn't in a coven.

More years went by. I was lucky enough to actually *find* a coven that seemed to fit me, and I learned a lot from my teachers and covenmates. But out in the wider community? I still wasn't considered a real witch. This time, it was because I wasn't in the *right* coven. We didn't have a traditional lineage that could be traced back to one of Wicca's original founders.

Well, poo!

As a young teenager, enthusiastically clutching fresh copies of Scott Cunningham and Silver RavenWolf, I was shocked to be called a "fluffy bunny" and told that I wasn't a "real" witch because I was too young and too inexperienced. Undeterred, I kept learning and practicing.

And here I am now, more years later still. I'm a third-degree priestess in what my covenmates jokingly call the "Wiccan mothership"—Gardnerian Wicca: the first Wiccan tradition, before *Wicca* was even the word for it—with lineage coming out of my ears. Our early leaders were some of the first public witches, and they inspired countless others through their writing and teaching.

And guess what? I *still* have people who tell me I'm not a real witch. Sometimes they say it's because my tradition was "made up" in the twentieth century. It's not *really* witchcraft, just watered-down New Age beliefs mixed with ceremonial magic and feel-good self-help. Other times it's because I strive to follow a moral code that discourages baneful magic. Real witches aren't afraid to curse, and do so freely. Real witches are scary. They're transgressive, living on society's fringes. Real witches talk to the dead. Real witches are solitary. Real witches belong to the right covens. Real witches…You get the idea.

I just couldn't seem to get it right. I still can't. No matter what I do, there are other witches out there confidently expounding on all the reasons why people like me aren't "real" witches.

This kind of naysaying was hard for me to deal with as a youngster, but the truth is that I struggled with insecurity and the "realness" of my witchcraft well into adulthood. What if those people were right? What if I was doing it wrong? What if I really *didn't* have the right to call myself a witch? What if I was missing something, the way people (almost always on the internet) said I was? I usually played things pretty cool, but the issue ate at me in one form or another for years.

Imposter Syndrome

In other communities and disciplines, this nagging fear that you don't belong—that you're not really a member of the group and one day everyone else will figure it out and shun you—is called *imposter syndrome*. It's almost never actually based in reality, and it affects most people in one way or another at some point in their lives. It's not actually an indication of any kind of truth, but that doesn't make it any easier to deal with. In witchcraft communities—whether Wiccan, traditional, Luciferian, secular, or any other variety—imposter syndrome can be especially hard to deal with because we can be so critical of each other. Witchcraft is an intense, consuming practice that, even if we don't think of it as our religion, tends to become central to our identity over time. Witchcraft is a core part of who we are, and that means that even if we don't mean to, we tend to form very particular ideas about what it entails and what sorts of people are best suited to practice it. It hurts to be confronted by other paradigms that seem to threaten our own. It can be frustrating to meet people who don't seem to value things the way we do. It's especially jarring to be told directly that it's you who's got it wrong.

When it comes to matters of identity, nerves are raw from the get-go. Tempers flare quickly. Evolutionarily speaking, human beings are social animals, and our status as an insider or an outsider, on a primal level, can be a matter of survival. In these terms, it's easy to understand why the quest for authenticity—for realness—can get so heated. It's about *belonging*. And even the most solitary of us has to belong somewhere.

Among witches today, it's also about social power. As decentralized as witchcraft is, the Craft still has its celebrities. I grew in the Craft emulating authors: powerful people who seemed to make their witchcraft flow effortlessly through their lives. Now I know it's more complicated than that, but as a community, we still tend to look to writers to tell us how to do things properly. Today's witches also have Instagram, YouTube, and a half dozen other social media platforms, each with famous witches modeling what the Craft should look like (whether they mean to or not). And if someone has thousands of followers, their witchcraft must be worth emulating, right? And what does it say about us if our altars, our bookshelves, our ritual robes, or our tools don't look like theirs?

Many of us struggle at one time or another with feeling like our practice isn't what it's supposed to be. We may have been told that we're not really practicing witchcraft because we don't meet someone else's standards. Maybe the things we see in our social media feeds make us feel inadequate. We feel like frauds, like we don't belong.

How to Combat Imposter Syndrome

So what can you do to combat imposter syndrome? How do you set aside the anxiety surrounding the question *Am I a real witch?*

First, understand that there's really no such thing as one most real, most authentic witchcraft. Just look at how the definition of *witch* changes according to who is using it. Over the centuries, wherever we look in the world, *witch* has meant something different to different people. No one has ever had exclusive ownership of the word. To some medieval Europeans, a witch was a person who had signed a contract with the devil and broken covenant with Christ. Depending on where you lived and what century you were living in, the witch more likely might have been a poor old woman on the outskirts of town, a wealthy man with land to be coveted, a disfigured child, or even an animal. Prior to the Middle Ages, the witch might have been thought of as a healer, a seeress, or someone with power beyond what the gods ascribed to other humans. In West Africa, India, and the Americas, we see even more examples across history, all of them unique.

In the contemporary world, many people believe witches to be practitioners of a gentle nature religion, or members of an initiatory cult, or New Age believers interested in ushering in the Aquarian Age. Male witches are reclaiming the word *warlock*, and young women are adopting the moniker *witch* to brand their businesses and proclaim their independence from the status quo. None of these definitions are wrong (not even the ones you don't like), because witchcraft has been (and still is) many of these things. It doesn't belong to any one group. So how can anyone say definitively what witchcraft is or isn't in such narrow terms? History is standing by to prove them wrong.

Second, know that there's no winning the debate over authenticity, no matter how hard you try. As my own story demonstrates, there will always be someone standing by to tell you you're doing things wrong. You can read every book on the shelves. You can go live off the land and commune with local spirits. You can be initiated into a formal coven by the oldest practitioners of a tradition. You can perform the most intense rituals that leave you absolutely convinced that you've seen the gods themselves. You can lead public rituals, build communities, and work magic that changes lives. But none of that matters, because the sort of person who finds fault and harps on it will find it regardless of what you do. If your Craft is important to you, then you have to do it anyway. There will always be people who are eager to tell you that you're not real, but only you can know that for sure. Don't give naysayers more of an audience than they deserve.

> **There will always be people who are eager to tell you that you're not real, but only you can know that for sure. Don't give naysayers more of an audience than they deserve.**

Finally, give the social-media witchcraft a rest. I'm not saying to get rid of your accounts, but find a way to give them less power over your life. Maybe that means setting time limits for how long you spend on your phone or computer, or maybe that means being choosier about whom you follow. Even if we don't do much interacting, just being constantly exposed to particular kinds of images and attitudes impacts us in very tangible ways. Psychologists and sociologists have been connecting the dots between media portrayals of women and body-image issues in young girls for decades now, and the same principles apply. We model ourselves after what we see, even when we're not aware of it. This can be a good thing. If you follow people who inspire you, challenge you to grow, and otherwise make you feel good, then that's awesome. But it's easy for envy to work its way in. It's easy to see someone else's Craft from afar and unconsciously decide that your own is lacking. Hey, my altars never look like what I see on Pinterest and Instagram either! Sometimes I see all those posts of people doing things for the full moon (or whatever) and I worry that I don't do enough ritual, or I feel bad for just not having the energy or time to totally witch out. But the reality is that people post their highlights. They post their good-hair days and their amazing trips and whatever expensive thing they just bought, but most people don't post much of the stuff in between. So it's not fair to compare your everyday practice with your internet highlight feed. Their witchcraft doesn't look like that all the time either!

We'll probably never get over the need to chase after "real" witchcraft, like something we can distill and sell. I think it's probably human nature to try to be special and to appear to our communities as though we've got it all figured out. However hard we may try, it's difficult to simply not care what other people think of us. But witchcraft isn't a stagnant thing that only belongs to one place or one people or one time period. It's diverse and flexible and takes on the character of the people who practice it. Your witchcraft—even if you belong to a tradition—won't look exactly like anyone else's. And wouldn't it be better for everyone if we stopped pretending that it should?

Thorn Mooney *is the author of* Traditional Wicca: A Seeker's Guide, *as well as a columnist for* Witches & Pagans *magazine and a blogger for Patheos Pagan. A Gardnerian priestess and coven leader, Thorn has been active in witch and Pagan communities for more than twenty years. She lives in North Carolina, where she works as a public school teacher, fights with swords, and plays guitar. Visit her at www.thornthewitch.com.*

Keeping Pagan Ways During the Holidays

James Kambos

The tension begins to build right around Labor Day. Walk into any large home-improvement store at that time and there they are—Christmas decorations! You'll see artificial Christmas trees decorated to the hilt. You'll see aisles of lights, garland, ornaments, and lawn decorations shaped like snowmen and reindeer. As autumn moves past Halloween, the big Christmas push turns into a frenzy. In every form of media—radio, print, television, and online—we are bombarded with ads for holiday decorating and gift giving. It seems like the media and their advertisers are trying to tell us that if we aren't ready for Christmas by Thanksgiving, we're slackers.

On top of that, on every street we hear that angst-filled question: *Are you ready?*

Hold on. Am I ready for *what?* And what the hell happened to peace on earth?

In December, many Witches and Pagans celebrate the Winter Solstice, also known as Yule. This is supposed to be a time of joy and gratefulness. The sun's power begins to increase, and the span of daylight begins to grow. Hope is restored.

It seems that many of the simple early Pagan beliefs enjoyed centuries ago at this time of year have been forgotten. What's sad is that many of today's holiday traditions are rooted in early Pagan customs. This is our holiday season too.

So how do we keep Pagan ways during the holidays?

Let's take a look at some of the issues Pagans face at this time of year. We'll also look at ways to keep our cool and stay balanced during this hectic season.

Many Faiths and Traditions

During December, many religions and faiths have major religious and cultural celebrations. There is Hanukkah, Yule, Christmas, and Kwanzaa. Most of us truly want to connect with the positive values and meanings these holidays focus on, such as family, sharing, generosity, and kindness. But the hectic pace of the season, the demands of work and family, and the financial stress the holidays can bring may cause frazzled nerves and make tempers snap.

For Pagans, the stress of dealing with the holidays can be a trickier situation than for most. Many Pagans were raised in Christian families. So many of them did, and some still do, celebrate Christmas, and that's okay. Some Pagans, however, observe Yule instead. But even if you're Pagan and observe only Yule, during the holidays you're almost bound to come into contact with family and friends who do observe Christmas. At work also, you'll probably attend a holiday party of some sort. Additionally, if you're Pagan and have any parties at your home, your guest list may easily include non-Pagans. So being Pagan at this time of year isn't easy, but it can be done.

When Pagans and non-Pagans gather for holiday festivities, the stress level can be double because both groups may tend to think about their differences rather than their similarities.

As Pagans, we tend to be more magically inclined than the general population. Now is the time that we need to use that magic more than ever. It will help us maintain our Pagan ways and keep our equilibrium during this frantic time of year. Don't let the holiday hoopla make you neglect your magic or your spirituality. By working your magic, you'll help create a happy holiday atmosphere for everyone you encounter. Besides that, you may even find a little peace on earth for yourself and those you love.

Daily Protection Magic

I've found that doing a little protection magic each day is the key to helping create a low-stress, pleasant holiday season. When you perform protection magic, you're creating a shield of protective energy that will surround you all day. You can also visualize a protective shield as needed and draw it around you during a stressful situation. This type of magic will be with you as you navigate a busy parking lot looking for a spot or when dealing with an overwhelmed sales associate, and it will even be with you when the office Christmas party gets out of hand.

Here is what I do. I begin each day with protection magic in the form of *words of power* accompanied by visualizations. This will ground and center you. You may charge yourself and your living space with words such as these: "There is one power. The power is perfect protection, and I am a perfect manifestation of this power."

As you speak your intention, visualize yourself, anyone else you want to protect, your home, or your car. Then raise your power hand and turn clockwise. As you do this, in your mind's eye, see a stream of white light radiating from your hand. See this light sealing anyone or anything you wish with a protective aura.

As you go about your day, if you should encounter a challenging situation or a negative person, "see" that same protective aura surrounding you. You'll be surprised at how it will neutralize any negative energy coming your way. At the same time, it will ground you and help you remain calm.

Another easy way to protect yourself from holiday stress is to perform a short, simple altar devotional. All you'll need are a few minutes and a favorite candle. Light the candle safely and sit before it. Gaze at the flame and see its glow grow until you're surrounded by its warmth. Think or whisper, "Perfect calm. Perfect peace." Repeat the words until you really do feel calm. Then snuff out the candle, return to an everyday state of mind, and resume your daily routine.

To extend your level of protection magic and make it more mobile, consider turning a favorite piece of jewelry into a protective charm. For example, it may be a pendant shaped like a magical symbol, such as a pentagram or an eye of Horus. But it doesn't need to be in the shape of a traditional magical symbol. It could be a favorite charm, pendant, or ring that once belonged to a relative. To charge it, take the piece of jewelry in your hand, hold it to your heart, then say, "Perfect charm, protect me from all harm." Now wear it whenever you wish, especially to holiday gatherings.

With any protection magic, using either the ideas I've given here or protection magic of your choosing, what we are doing is drawing a line. We are saying to ourselves that we are centering our physical and spiritual bodies inside a protective barrier. We are keeping out unwanted negative energy; it can't bother us because we don't want it to. "Seeing" your protective shield when you're faced with a negative situation during the holidays will keep you centered. Using these visualizations will help keep you from reacting in an unhealthy way. You'll be much less likely to be drawn into any family drama.

The beautiful thing is that no one needs to know you're keeping the peace by using your magical Pagan ways.

When you work a little protection magic each day, it won't just keep you centered but will also prepare you to face the holiday season.

Now when someone asks you "Are you ready?" you can say *yes!*

Holiday Candle and Fire Magic

Fire in any form is a beautiful and subtle way to practice your Pagan faith and spirituality during the holidays without attracting a lot of attention. Burning candles and a crackling fire are enjoyed by people of all religions and spiritual backgrounds, so you may enjoy performing some fire magic during the holidays when you're alone or while you have company—and no one needs to know. Using fire while you have guests is also a good magical way to create a calm atmosphere.

Here are some tips on how to magically charge your candles or fires before company arrives. To magically charge your candles, anoint each candle with a drop of olive oil. Rub the oil up and down each candle. As you do this, think or say *peace* at least three times. Another way to charge your candles is to place all the candles you are going to use on a table or an altar. Sprinkle around them some dried peace-attracting herb, such as lavender. Leave them undisturbed for about a day, then discard the herb you used and use the candles as you wish.

If you don't have time to charge your candles before a holiday ritual or before guests arrive, I suggest keeping at least two bayberry-scented candles on hand. Their scent is well known for attracting peace and good fortune. They're perfect for Pagan rituals or for family gatherings.

For those of you with fireplaces, burn the following woods for holiday magic. Oak can be used to represent the God at Yule or any time. Beech will draw the force of the Goddess. For an all-purpose good-luck wood, burn ash. If, for some reason, you're expecting trouble at a planned holiday family event at your home, sprinkle some mistletoe in the fire before guests arrive. It's a good all-around protection herb.

Deck the Halls

For Pagans, it's easy to keep our Pagan ways and show our faith as we do our holiday decorating. Most of the modern Christmas/holiday decorations in use today have Pagan roots. Before Christianity existed, Pagans were decorating at Yule with greenery and exchanging small gifts.

Today's holiday decor is rich with Pagan symbolism. When you decorate your home at this time of year, you're probably already using a Pagan-inspired theme. Here are some things to think about so you understand the Pagan origins of today's holiday decorations.

The greenery we use today—the Yule tree, the garland, the swags—are symbols of eternity. Early Pagans looked with awe at the evergreens in the winter landscape. Everything else appeared dead, but the noble evergreens stood green with life against the snow. The round wreath you may use is also Pagan-inspired, and it too symbolizes eternity. The color red in holiday decor is also of Pagan origin. It represents the life force.

Nut- and fruit-shaped ornaments come from Pagans too. They serve to remind us of the bounty and blessings of the harvest. Holly was also handed down to us by early Pagans. It was brought into the home at Yule for good luck.

As the year draws to a close and both Christians and Pagans decorate, we should all pause to reflect on our common bonds instead of our differences.

Good will to all and—yes, even I have to say it—peace on earth.

James Kambos *is a writer and an artist from Ohio. He's written many articles and essays about Appalachian and Middle Eastern folk traditions. He has also designed cards and calendars. He holds a degree in history and geography from Ohio University.*

Ethical Love Spells

Deborah Lipp

It's typical to hear that love spells are unethical. In Wicca, "don't do love spells" is a common piece of advice, and many other traditions concur. Googling today, I found many reasons for this, including "it's bad karma," "there are no good outcomes," "it robs the other person of free will," and that old standby, "be careful what you wish for."

All of these are true. The rise of consent culture merely underlines that Wicca has been, ethically, ahead of the curve. While the current conversation about consent seems new and trendy to many mainstream people, in Wicca we've been saying for decades that it's wrong to usurp another's free will. All parties in a relationship must choose that relationship freely.

In addition to spells that interfere with free will, there's another, less discussed type of love spell that is unethical: It is unethical to work magic designed to break a vow or an oath. A vow is, itself, an act of magic: a person gives their word, often before God or gods, and transmutes that word into a bond. To work magic in direct violation of that—whether the oath is yours or another's—is a bad idea. The assumption when making an oath is that you have asked the gods to align their will with yours, so to work magic against it is, in a sense, to go against these gods. Not to mention it goes against the basic honesty and integrity inherent in taking a vow.

While the current conversation about consent seems new and trendy to many mainstream individuals, in Wicca we've been saying for decades that it is wrong to usurp another's free will. All parties in a relationship must choose that relationship freely.

Some people, once they've said that some or all love magic is wrong, will go on to invoke the threefold law (a variation on the "bad karma" argument), but I feel that is unnecessary. If you understand it's wrong to do something, it should not matter whether or not there are also negative consequences. I hope, reader, that you are the type of person who will refuse to do something morally wrong even if there are no consequences at all!

And if you're not such a person, keep in mind that magic brings more of the self to bear than does mundane action. Magic makes both the direct results and the side effects more intense. Magic and mundane activity both deal with behavior, but magic also deals with the soul. Which is to say, if you are cheating on your spouse, so be it, but don't use magic to help the infidelity along.

By the way, everything here applies whether you're working to bring love into your own life or doing spells on behalf of someone else. For the sake of simplicity, I'll assume you're working to find love for yourself from here on out.

Love Goals and Love Targets

It's not that love spells are unethical. It's that certain premises for love spells are unethical, particularly those dependent upon unethical outcomes.

Magic spells are an activity intended to achieve an outcome. That is, spells have goals. The more specific the goal, the more effective the spell. If your goal is unethical, your spell is unethical.

I think we can all agree that "finding love" is a perfectly ethical goal. What's unacceptable is a goal like "I will be with so-and-so, whether he/she/they wants to be with me or not." Often, the person performing such a spell will phrase it in a nicer-sounding way. "He and I belong together; he just doesn't realize it yet" is typical. But such phrasing still disregards the consent of the other person. When we're besotted, the basic truth that others get to choose whether or not to be with us is sometimes too painful to acknowledge. Surely the other person must be confused/deluded/in denial. But they have that choice, and we don't get to use magic to take away that choice.

In my 2017 book *Magical Power for Beginners*, I spend a lot of time talking about the difference between a magical goal and a magical target:

> [Goals] are *why* you do magic. They are not *where* you send power.
>
> Imagine that you practice archery, and you are trying to win a medal. The goal is the medal. The target is the round thing with the bull's-eye on it. It's very important that you shoot your arrow at the target and not at the goal—if you shoot the arrow at the goal, you might hit a judge, and that would be bad (161).

When you do a spell, raise power while imagining the goal and then send that power to the target. For ethical love magic, we need to explore both ethical goals and ethical targets.

We've established that an *unethical* goal is to capture the love of another regardless of their free will. It is as wrong to *magically* force someone into your bed as it is to *physically* force them. In fact, it's worse.

ETHICAL LOVE GOALS

An ethical goal respects consent, is for the good of all, and breaks no vows. Here are some examples of ethical love goals:

- To bring love into my life
- To find my soul mate
- To increase my attractiveness
- To be in the right place at the right time
- To open connection and communication

These are goals that meet basic ethical standards and, when used in a well-constructed spell, could change your life for the better.

ETHICAL LOVE TARGETS

An ethical love spell also sends the energy to an appropriate target. There are three possible targets for a love spell:

• Yourself

• "Fate"

• A potential partner

Each of these deserves some more discussion.

Everyone can agree that targeting yourself is entirely ethical. If you set aside magic, you can see that most of what we do to find love in life, we do by targeting ourselves. This involves everything from getting a makeover, to wearing clothes and colognes designed to be attractive, to creating online profiles, to reading self-help books in the hope of transforming consciousness and overcoming obstacles to love.

Magic is another way of targeting the self. Looking at the goals we listed, we would target the self to bring love generally or to make ourselves more attractive. Spells to become attractive are called *glamours*. Specifically, they're designed to draw people to whom you are attracted—although they can work *too* well. A friend of mine worked a simple glamour and had four offers in a single weekend, which was a bit overwhelming (but fun).

Spells to become attractive are called *glamours*. Specifically, they're designed to draw people to whom you are attracted—although they can work *too* well. A friend of mine worked a simple glamour and had four offers in a single weekend.

A *Simple Glamour*

Do this spell outside, during a full moon, preferably on a clear night when you can see moonlight.

Rub seven drops of rose water on a piece of rose quartz, saying with each drop, "Moon of love, moon of love, draw love wherever I go."

Leave the quartz exposed to moonlight overnight.

Carry or wear the quartz thereafter.

. . . .

"Fate" is a tricky concept, which is why I put the word in quotes. You may not believe there is such a thing. But there are still a lot of intangibles that surround us, and magic is good at aligning those intangibles in a way that works in our favor. To meet the woman of your dreams at a bus stop, you'd both have to leave home at the right time to catch the same bus and have enough of a wait to catch each other's eye. Intangibles can be as diverse as the weather, how you responded when the alarm went off, whether or not you had to stop and feed the cat, whether your feet hurt, etc. We can lump any and all of these things under "fate," or "the gods," or "synchronicity."

Fate is your target for right-place/right-time goals or meeting your soul mate. You can replace "fate" with a deity, with your own higher self, with your guardian angel, or any other such concept that works for you. The following spell uses fate.

A *Soul Mate Spell*

Consecrate two flowers: one for yourself and one for a love you have yet to meet (your soul mate). Place each in a vase at opposite ends of your altar, saying, "Fate, bring us together."

Move the vases closer together every night for five nights, repeating each time, "Fate, bring us together." Concentrate deeply as you do so.

On the sixth night, place both flowers in the same vase and say, "Fate brings us together."

On the seventh night, twist the stems of the flowers together. Take the flowers to a source of natural running water (a stream or river is ideal) and drop them in, saying, "Fate brings us together."

The flowing water represents fate carrying the two of you to an unknown, intertwined future.

Targeting Other People

What about targeting a potential partner? If the partner is unknown to you, then the appropriate target is fate/a deity/etc. You can't clearly target the unknown, so an intermediary of some kind is called for.

But what about a known person? Most people would immediately recoil from this or, contrarily, would leap in without regard to ethics. But is there an ethical way to do love magic on another person?

This is a personal decision, obviously. Some people are very strict about it, and say that *any* magic done on another person, without that person's permission, is immoral. I am not someone who shares that opinion. When we do anything—magical or mundane—that affects others without their explicit consent, we have to be very careful about our ethics. But a strict "no, never" is a way of avoiding complex ethical decision making.

Here are some broad examples. Most people would agree that you could perform CPR on an unconscious person even though they aren't able to consciously consent. Similarly, you could perform life-saving acts on an infant. The police can arrest and courts can try a murderer or thief despite their lack of consent. In each of these cases, there's a compelling reason to act: out of concern for the life or well-being of the subject or others.

What about good wishes? Now we're in murky territory. We all have encountered that one person who is just too helpful, whose help is more intrusive than appreciated. Consider prayer. Not everyone is comfortable being prayed for. Christians who think Pagans are demonic don't want us invoking gods for them, while many Pagans don't want Christians praying for them, especially prayers that are intended to convert.

Despite these exceptions, most goodwill is appreciated, harmless, and ethical. The fact that ethics should be questioned and considered in a given situation doesn't mean that situation is a hard *no*.

You cannot ethically compel someone to love you. Imagining the non-magical equivalent will bring up images of mind control, if not rape and kidnapping, so you can easily understand the prohibition. But what could you do, non-magically, to influence someone you desire?

Opening communication, increasing awareness, and removing barriers between you and another all could target your potential partner ethically. The other person would have 100 percent free choice about being with you.

You could open a line of communication by sending flirty or friendly messages. You could find out what that person is interested in and find out more about it so you'll have something to talk about. You could find out that person's favorite hangout and stop by. (I don't mean stalking, obviously. Back when people didn't have cell phones, "stopping by" was much more common and raised no eyebrows.)

Magically, some of this could be accomplished with fate-oriented, right-place/right-time spells or with a glamour. But opening communication, increasing awareness, and removing barriers between you and another all could target your potential partner ethically. The other person would have 100 percent free choice about being with you but would make this decision while aware of you, with lines of communication open, and/or with barriers removed.

A *Spell to Open Communication*

With a picture of your beloved (or potential beloved) before you, visualize your throat chakra. Visualize bright light pouring from it. Using bright royal-blue body paint or some other kind of paint that is safe to use on the body, paint your throat area blue while continuing to visualize.

Now visualize bright light pouring from your beloved's throat chakra. While holding this image clearly in your mind, paint the picture so that your beloved's throat is bright blue too.

Visualize the two streams of bright blue light connecting with each other, so that the two of you are able to speak freely.

Now simply begin speaking, saying all the things you wish you could say, while continuing to visualize the light.

When you are finished and are ready to wash your throat, leave a speck of blue under the jawline, where it won't be visible. Leave the picture of your beloved on your altar.

· · · · · · · · · · · · ·

As magical practitioners, we have to monitor ourselves closely because we can go overboard. If we're in love or infatuated, it's easy to lie to ourselves. We can go too far when we want something or someone very badly. We can tell ourselves that we're doing an ethical spell to open communication when we're really constructing a manipulative, harmful spell. If you're not sure of yourself, refrain from magic.

I've gotten around this obstacle by working with others. I've traded love spells with another witch—she worked for me to find love, and

I worked for her. I was able to work ethically for her, and she for me, because the intensity of our desires didn't blind us.

By carefully choosing our goal and target, by respecting the free will of others, honoring oaths, and reaching out for help when we need it, we can create love magic that is as ethical as it is effective.

Deborah Lipp's *most recent books are* Magical Power for Beginners *and* Tarot Interactions. *Her earlier works include* The Study of Witchcraft, The Elements of Ritual, The Way of Four, The Way of Four Spellbook, Merry Meet Again, *and* The Ultimate James Bond Fan Book. *One of these things is not like the other.*

Deborah has been teaching Wicca, magic, and the occult for over thirty years. She became a Witch and a High Priestess in the 1980s, as an initiate of the Gardnerian tradition of Wicca. She's been published in many Pagan publications, including newWitch, Llewellyn's Magical Almanac, Pangaia, *and* Green Egg, *and has lectured on Pagan and occult topics on three continents.*

*As an active "out of the closet" member of the Pagan community, Deborah has appeared in various media discussing Wicca, including Coast-to-Coast radio, an A&E documentary (*Ancient Mysteries: Witchcraft in America*), television talk shows, and the* New York Times.

In "real life," Deborah is a business analyst. She lives with her spouse, Melissa, and an assortment of cats in Jersey City, NJ, three blocks from a really great view of Freedom Tower. Deborah reads and teaches Tarot, solves and designs puzzles, watches old movies, hand-paints furniture, and dabbles in numerous handcrafts.

Follow Deborah on Twitter: @DebLippAuthor.

Building Bridges: How to Design Interfaith Rituals

Elizabeth Barrette

The world is full of religions of all varieties. When members of different religions come together for causes or events, we call that *interfaith* work. Many Pagan groups include members of different traditions—our *eclectic* circles. Groups of a single tradition, such as a Wiccan coven or a Druidic grove, may join together for major sabbats or other activities such as a Pagan picnic. Most Pagans have relatives who belong to some other faith(s). Therefore, some events, such as handfastings, may involve people of other religions. Ideally, events with a mix of attendees should offer interfaith activities that appeal to a wide range of participants and minimize the chance of annoying anyone.

Why Do Interfaith Rituals?

There are many reasons why people choose to hold events for mixed traditions. Sometimes it's the only option. Most often, it's incidental—they want to do something and the participants have an assortment of faiths, so the suggestions and development wind up mixed as well. Other times, people design an interfaith activity for the specific purpose of mingling. This tends to work better when done deliberately, with an eye toward balancing different needs and tastes.

One key reason for interfaith design is that if you *don't* do it when you have a mixed crowd, the results tend to suck. Most of us have attended an event, often at somebody else's church, where the hosts were downright oppressive and disrespectful toward everyone outside their own faith. That's a great way to kill friendships, start fights, and drive people away from your religion.

When you design an interfaith event and do a good job, it incorporates motifs from all participating religions. This shows people more about how other traditions work, which improves their understanding of members of that faith. They recognize things that are similar to their own practices and realize that we all have a lot in common.

This promotes tolerance. The more people know about each other's beliefs and practices, the better they tend to put up with differences. Interfaith events therefore promote tolerance at a time when the world really needs to work on that virtue instead of picking fights with everyone who is different.

Tolerance leads to peace. When people understand each other better and tolerate each other more, they feel less aggressive and more benevolent. This encourages them to choose nonviolent methods of

resolving conflict. Planning an interfaith event gives you a chance to practice this when the inevitable disputes come up. Once you've done that, it becomes easier to smooth ruffled feathers at the event itself.

As a result, interfaith rituals provide an excellent opportunity to teach the skills of peacemaking. First, the organizers can model peaceful methods when mishaps occur. Second, you can smooth the way for attendees by explaining what to expect, how to choose between options, and how to accommodate differences. A little introduction like that is plenty for a handfasting or other small to medium event. If you're hosting a Pagan picnic or other large event with programming, then consider offering a presentation on interfaith issues and peacemaking.

Interfaith rituals provide an excellent opportunity to teach the skills of peacemaking. First, the organizers can model peaceful methods when mishaps occur. Second, you can smooth the way for attendees by explaining what to expect, how to choose between options, and how to accommodate differences.

Diversity makes the world more interesting. Interfaith rituals are appealing because they contain things that are new and exciting for most people. Diversity also improves problem-solving potential. The more different perspectives you have, the greater the chance that at least one of those people will spot a solution. If you're lucky, several people will offer ideas and you can pick the best one. If you have only one perspective and a solution is not visible from there, then you're out of luck. This is especially true with religions, because each one is good at different things.

Overall, inclusivity supports stronger ties of family and community. It helps people see that they have more in common than they have differences. In a world plagued by divisive politics and violent conflicts, inclusivity builds bridges. When we form alliances between different religions, we benefit from strength in numbers. This especially benefits minority religions. For example, you'll see Jews sticking up for Pagans' right to wear a pentacle, and Pagans chipping in to fix up a mosque after vandalism. We are stronger together than apart. Interfaith rituals support and celebrate that.

Key Concepts

Within the context of interfaith activities, certain key concepts come up. Organizers need to account for these when planning an event. This forethought offers the best chance of success.

REPRESENTATION

Which religions are likely to be present at the event? Knowing this in advance will help you decide which motifs to use or to avoid. Handfastings often have a dual focus: the bride's family follows one religion and the groom's family another. Public events tend to be more random because anyone could show up, but you can estimate the likely attendees just by looking at the type of event and the local demographics of common religions. At a Pagan picnic, you're more likely to wind up juggling a mix of Asatru, Druids, and Wiccans.

AFFINITY

Which groups tend to get along or get into fights? Some faiths, such as Buddhism, have strong traditions of nonviolence and thus have a low rate of conflict. Others, such as Asatru, attract and encourage assertive people; if they get hassled, they're more prone to push back. Consider current conflicts, like the rising problem of Islamophobia, and historic ones, like Pagans and Christians tending to rub each other the wrong way. Use this awareness to reduce tension. For instance, seating the Buddhists between the Pagans and the Christians has a lower chance of conflict than putting the Pagans and the Christians beside each other.

OVERLAP

What things are the same or not? Any two or more groups will have a range of commonalities versus differences. Effective interfaith work relies a great deal on identifying shared motifs and practices. Ideally, you want a lot of common ground on which to build a stable foundation, with interesting differences sprinkled throughout to catch people's attention. Learn to watch for elements that appear in many traditions, such as music or candles.

AVERSIONS

What do people find annoying? This is one of the most challenging factors in creating a good interfaith event. Some people really love doing things that other people find boring or downright aggravating. Christians adore saying "Jesus," but many Pagans dislike hearing it, especially a lot of it. Most Pagans love magic, but many other people feel uncomfortable with it. Interfaith work often involves modulating the heavier elements to a more symbolic level to avoid bothering people. Remember that the goal is for everyone to have a good time!

ANTAGONISTS

How will you deal with difficult individuals? Some people's religious mode of thought is "my way or the highway." If that person is a primary celebrant, such as the bride or groom, or is paying for the event, like the bride's parents, then you may need to let them have their way on major points and use interfaith means to buffer the effects in other places. If the antagonist is *not* a primary celebrant or donor, then they have much less influence. Remind them that group activities often entail compromise. It helps to assign some of your more mellow people to be ushers so they can step in to smooth ruffled feathers if necessary. Also include space where people can get away from each other. Bear in mind that alcohol lowers inhibitions and can increase aggression. Some religions use it, while others forbid it. Just omitting intoxicants can reduce the tension and the chance of a serious fight breaking out.

It helps to assign some of your more mellow people to be ushers so they can step in to smooth ruffled feathers if necessary. Also include space where people can get away from each other.

Ritual Options

What are the choices available to attendees? Many religions have certain practices that are only offered to, or are primarily desired by, members of their own faith. Obviously this leaves out people of other faiths, which in a mixed context is not good. Most of these problems can be solved by offering attendees multiple ways to participate. I went to a (primarily Christian) funeral where attendees had the option of receiving communion, receiving a nondenominational blessing, or staying seated, and if you went up, you indicated which you wanted by how you held your arms. I also went to a (primarily Pagan) handfasting where attendees had the option of joining in call-and-response lines, just holding a lit stick of incense, or sitting without doing either. Those are discreet and elegant arrangements that give most people something they feel comfortable doing.

How to Design an Interfaith Ritual

The steps for creating an interfaith ritual or other event are similar to those for event planning in general. You just need some extra steps to accommodate the differences. It is easier to do this as you go along, rather than writing a single-faith ritual and then trying to adapt it after the fact. If you're designing a ritual for a very common theme, such as a handfasting or a funeral, there are books and other materials to help you organize your planning process.

First, consider the topic of the event. Are you planning a sabbat ritual, a house blessing, a handfasting, or what? Some types of ritual relate to universal life experiences (birth, death, etc.) and thus have parallels across most or all religions. Others (holidays, devotions to specific deities, etc.) are more particular and the details may diverge widely.

Second, estimate the probable religions that will be participating. Sometimes you will know this exactly, but other times you just have to guess. The more you know about the faiths likely to attend, the better you can tailor your ritual to appeal to your audience. Related religions (such as several branches of Paganism, or several monotheistic faiths arising from the Middle East) are easier to

Estimate the probable religions that will be participating. Sometimes you will know this exactly, but other times you just have to guess. The more you know about the faiths likely to attend, the better you can tailor your ritual to appeal to your audience. Related religions … are easier to match up than those stemming from radically different origins.

match up than those stemming from radically different origins. If you have a very high degree of diversity, it gets difficult to appeal to everyone. In this case, look for universal human experiences and practices that appear in the greatest number of traditions, such as candles.

Next, examine how each of those religions handles the topic at hand. What makes someone "married" in Wicca, in Christianity, or in Judaism? What tools do they use? What actions do they perform? Are there key words or phrases that must be said? Of the many customs that accrue, which are essential and which are basically window dressing? It helps to write down notes sorted by topic, such as supplies and liturgy.

Now is a good time to ask for ideas from people who plan to attend. This is essential for some rituals, such as a coming-of-age ceremony, where one or a few key people need to feel satisfied in order for it to qualify as a success. In any case, though, getting input raises your chance of success. This is especially true when you're trying to incorporate elements of a tradition you don't personally practice. People who belong to that faith will suggest things you wouldn't think of doing and can help you prioritize the more important motifs.

With this information in hand, you can identify common ground. Look for similarities in tools, colors, symbolism, and so on. If nothing else, rituals all have a beginning, a middle, and an end; often there are parallels in marking those stages. At the same time, consider potential conflicts or special needs. Some religions tend to keep people moving around a lot, while others leave them seated. A mobility impairment that is negligible in a Christian church (which involves a lot of sitting and occasional kneeling) may be a burden in a mosque (where prayers involve a lot of up-and-down motion) and downright incompatible with a spiral dance (which requires at least several minutes of continuous full-body motion). Here is where you rule out things that appeal to one group but repel another. Roasting a sacred pig for a handfasting feast will not work if half the crowd is Jewish or Muslim, and if most participants are not Christian, then communion might be better saved for a denominational event. Remember to provide options! You can avoid a lot of stress by letting people choose what to do. Incompatible motifs can often be offered in separate areas.

Next, choose a framework. To do this, look at examples from each of your featured traditions. Ideally, try to find a framework that has similar versions in each source. If the infrastructure is too different, however, another option is to use the framework of one tradition with the trappings of another. For instance, Wicca has a very flexible ritual pattern that involves calling quarters, casting a circle, invok-

Remember to provide options! You can avoid a lot of stress by letting people choose what to do…. Next, choose a framework. To do this, look at examples from each of your featured traditions. Ideally, try to find a framework that has similar versions in each source.

ing higher powers, performing the main body of the ritual, and then releasing each part in reverse order. Into that you can put invocations and symbols for whichever deities your participants worship.

After that, fill most of the framework with common motifs. This helps people feel comfortable. Then add a few divergences, making sure to include something from each tradition. Look for the "cool" things that outsiders rarely get to see and will remember fondly. On the one hand, you have motifs that appear in many religions, such as candles and singing. On the other, you have motifs that appear in few religions or only one, which means that people who don't belong to that tradition probably haven't seen it before. Examples of the latter include jumping the broom in Pagan weddings and breaking the glass in Jewish ones. Work in explanations and instructions. Interfaith rituals need a lot more of this because people can't just follow a familiar path taken from a single religion, and this helps them find that common ground.

Once you have a rough draft, review the complete outline of your interfaith ritual. Make sure you haven't left out anything important.

If possible, seek feedback from other people. For key events like a handfasting or a funeral, you need approval from the main celebrants. Otherwise, it still helps to share the outline to avoid missteps.

Finally, polish the ritual one last time. Make any requested changes and proofread the whole thing. Then it's ready to print out and distribute.

. . . .

Designing an effective ritual for interfaith audiences is challenging but possible. These are learned skills, and you will get better with practice. It's best to start small, if you can, and grow from there. Jumping right into the deep end can be quite daunting. However, most Pagans will need to do an interfaith ritual at least once, so it's a good set of skills to acquire. Look for opportunities in your area so you can try your hand at this. You might be surprised by what you find!

Elizabeth Barrette *has been involved with the Pagan community for more than twenty-nine years. She served as managing editor of PanGaia for eight years and as dean of studies at the Grey School of Wizardry for four years. She has written columns on beginning and intermediate Pagan practice, Pagan culture, and Pagan leadership. Her book* Composing Magic: How to Create Magical Spells, Rituals, Blessings, Chants, and Prayers *explains how to combine writing and spirituality. She lives in central Illinois, where she has done much networking with Pagans in her area, such as coffeehouse meetings and open sabbats. Her other public activities include Pagan picnics and science fiction conventions. Visit her blog,* The Wordsmith's Forge *(https://ysabetwordsmith.dreamwidth.org/), or her website,* PenUltimate Productions *(http://penultimateproductions.weebly.com/). Her coven site, which includes extensive Pagan materials, is* Greenhaven Tradition *(http://greenhaventradition.weebly.com/).*

Magical Self-Care

NURTURE YOUR BODY, MIND & SPIRIT

Harness the Darkness: Strategies for Dealing With Depression

Rev. J. Variable x/ø

So you've got depression. Congratulations! You're a certified victim now, and you can bask in all the attention and sympathy that goes along with it.

Hang on. Hear me out.

For something that is such a downer, depression seems to be a popular disorder. According to a 2016 survey by the National Institute of Mental Health, 6.7 percent of adults in the United States are chronically depressed. Many more haven't been officially diagnosed, although they sure do take a lot of online psychological quizzes that assure them that they're miserable. Plug the term "depression" into your search engine and prepare for a barrage of articles promising to tell you how to overcome depression and get happy for good.

This is not one of those articles.

I am not a professional therapist. I don't know the details of your life or what you may be facing. I have, however, been living with depression for almost five decades, and I've learned a few tricks that have helped me stay on top of it. The condition runs on both sides of my family. I grew up with two depressive parents, back in the days when mental illness was a shameful secret. It took a long time for me to realize that it was not normal, not my fault, and not obligatory. I worked (and am still working) my way through it every day, without medication, on my own.

Here are some of the techniques I've learned that have kept me alive and appreciative of my existence. Perhaps you or someone you know will find them useful.

The Thing We Don't Talk About

I will now say a Very Bad Word: SUICIDE.

Yep, let's just get it out of the way right now. After all, it's not the climax of the story; it's an ever-present challenge throughout the narrative. This taboo subject still makes many people all squirmy and uncomfortable, but dragging it out into the open and talking about it isn't going to automatically send anyone off a cliff. Holding it in, feeling scared and ashamed: *that* is the danger.

I've lost my mother and three friends (so far) to suicide, and I've had a few close calls of my own. Even on good days, I often find myself fantasizing about how peaceful it would be to just check out.

Those with suicidal thoughts are told that they have to reach out for help, that they're not alone…but that's not always true, is it? It's nice to have a support group or a good friend to listen to you air out your darkest thoughts, but sometimes you *are* all alone. Sometimes, no matter how many people care about you, there's no one around when you really need them. Sometimes, even if they're right there, they just don't listen. Or you just can't talk.

On those days, you have to face depression in solitude.

You've got to save yourself.

Why?

Hell, I don't know. I'm not here to moralize or tell you what you've got to live for or to present a summary of all the different cultural views on suicide around the world. I don't know. I just know that no matter how far down I go, I always bounce back up, and I don't want to miss the next good day. We all die eventually anyway—it's not an option. All of this will be over soon enough, whether or not we're looking forward to it, and that idea can be strangely comforting. It helps me stay determined to hang around and make the best of it for a little longer, and then a little longer after that.

If you're going to survive depression, you need something (not someone) to hold onto. What's worked for you so far? Be honest. There are no wrong answers.

To Medicate or Not?

A few years ago, I went to the doctor because my arm hurt. He asked me how things were going in general, and I mentioned that I'd been feeling kind of down. His face brightened—actually *brightened*—and he offered to write me a prescription for a popular antidepressant right there on the spot.

My job at the time involved reviewing confidential information and studies from legal cases against certain pharmaceutical companies. I knew that some companies enticed doctors to push their products on patients, and that this particular medication often came with some truly horrific physical and mental side effects.

I refused the prescription. The doctor was disappointed.

Now, I'm not suggesting that all doctors are unscrupulous or that all medication is bad or unhelpful. I know people who absolutely cannot function without it. If you need it, take it. If it helps, great. I am saying that some doctors are all too willing to pass out pills like candy, and this sometimes does more harm than good. Find a doctor who has your best interests at heart, and don't hesitate to do some research on your own to see what medical professionals have to say about any given medication.

Watch Your Language

"I *suffer from* depression." Well, no kidding. It's not exactly a picnic in the park. But just like in spellcasting, words have power, so choose them carefully. When you say that you "suffer from" anything, you invoke the condition of suffering, essentially reinforcing to yourself and everyone else the idea that you're trapped, rubbing that version of reality deeper and deeper into your psyche. How about saying "I *have* depression" or "I *deal with* depression"? That imparts the same information without adding the extra tragedy juice.

Cancel the Pity Party

Let's admit it: as painful and real as depression is, it has some superficially attractive features. There's a familiar script to follow. If you talk about how bad you feel, people are supposed to listen and express sympathy. You get to be in the spotlight as everyone tries to build you up, and anyone who doesn't respond accordingly to your dramatic performance must be a heartless, uncaring excuse for a friend, giving you plenty of nice, chewy resentment that you can use as ammo for the next round.

Where do we draw the line between actual depression and plain old self-pity? They're so intertwined. Over and over, we're told that we need to express these feelings, to get them out in the open, to let our friends and family know that we're having a rough time. That's true. However, as hard as it may be to live *with* depression, living *beside* it is exhausting too.

Next time, before you call your friend to sit with you through another monologue of misery, ask yourself if you're actually looking for help or just an audience. Sometimes you really do need to just spew it out to a receptive ear. But if you find yourself spewing the same thing every week or every day, please, for the sake of your personal relationships, seek professional therapy. There are limits to what friends can do (or stand). No matter how much they love you, they didn't sign up for a front row seat to the daily Woe Is Me Show.

Spotting the Patterns

If you keep a journal, go back and study the thoughts you recorded during your depressive phases. It gets a bit repetitive, doesn't it? Your language and insights may have grown more sophisticated over time, but at its core, depression has a rather limited repertoire.

Set aside a little piece of your consciousness in an objective corner of your mind. Let this impartial observer take notes: "Ah, there's *that* thought again. And *that* one that always follows it. Hey, *that's* a new twist, but still the same basic concept." This clinical, nonjudgmental researcher gathers data and finds the patterns of stimuli and response. Later, when you're feeling better (and you know you will), you can review them. When the next episode comes around (and you know it will), it will be easier to recognize the markers and see each dark phase as just part of a cycle rather than an inescapable pit.

A Time for Wallowing

There will be times when you simply cannot ignore the sadness. Your impartial observer has gone to lunch and you're left alone, neck-deep in the mental muck.

Well, then, bring it on! Go ahead, marinade in the slop. Soak it up. Cry it out. Don't reason with it, contradict it, or tell it that it's overreacting. Coddle every awful thought as if it were a precious treasure. Give yourself permission to flail shamelessly in the depths of despair, with no hope of release.

But only for twenty minutes. That's it. No more, no less. When the time is up, you *must* rise, go wash your face, and find something else to do.

Happiness vs. Contentment

Depression loves to remind you that you aren't *happy*. It highlights every tiny disaster, everything you lack, every little way in which you don't measure up. And frequently it's not wrong—life *is* a struggle, and many dreams don't come true.

Guess what? Nobody's happy all the time. Nobody. Not really. Not even the people on magazine covers and in commercials. Not even your beautiful friend with the barf-inducingly positive social media profile. Break the habit of comparing yourself to others, and acknowledge the little things that are going right.

Happiness is fragile and fleeting; contentment is a solid foundation on which to build. It's immediately rewarding and demands nothing more than what you've already got.

Happiness is fragile and fleeting; contentment is a solid foundation on which to build. It's immediately rewarding and demands nothing more than what you've already got. Practice accepting each situation for what it is, including the aspects you're trying to change. Working toward your goals and being content in the moment are not mutually exclusive.

For every complaint that crosses your mind, find something pleasant to balance it out. Even if it's just appreciating a nice breeze through the window, a good song on the radio, or the fact that your lunch didn't make you sick. It takes practice and diligence and more than a little self-discipline, and it won't make depression disappear, but over time I promise you'll notice a big difference in your general outlook and emotional resilience.

Magical Therapy Session

We spend so much time and energy resisting depression, fighting against it, dreading its next visit. But alas, all the crystals, shielding, and positive thinking in the world won't help when the enemy is a part of you.

How about calling a truce?

Gather a collection of items that represent your best and worst moods. Get your journal out. Do whatever you do to prepare for magical work. When you're ready, invoke your depression and invite it to join you for a heart-to-heart. Ask it why it's here, what it wants, and how you might actually work together. Let it speak, without trying to judge or analyze. If it starts off sounding like a bully, consider that it might just be repeating your own assumptions. Wait for the "script" to run out, and eventually it will find its real voice.

Pay attention to the insights it has to offer and try to figure out with some ways that it can communicate with you more kindly. Resolve to hear it out. It's true that depression is a medical condition caused by chemical imbalances in the brain, but often, a low period is set off by misinterpretations of what's really happening in our environment, unrealistic expectations, or ignoring our own instincts. When your depression is focused on the idea that your life isn't going right, it could be that you're pushing too hard in the wrong direction.

Again, everything I've said here is based on my own personal experience. If my advice doesn't resonate with you, then keep looking for something that does. There is no quick, easy, or permanent fix for depression. It will most likely be your lifetime companion, in one form or another. It is not glamorous. It is not an opportunity to gaze, misty-eyed, into the shadows while everyone wonders about your terribly deep, tragic soul. It is not an all-purpose excuse. It sucks.

It is, however, only one part of your story. Don't let it become the main character. Pay attention and you can learn a lot about your own strengths from these patterns and work to change how they affect you.

Sources

National Institute of Mental Health. "Major Depression." Last updated November 2017. https://www.nimh.nih.gov/health/statistics/major-depression.shtml.

Rev. J. Variable x/ø *currently lives in Portland, Oregon, where she enjoys writing and arting in her spare time (and frequently when she really should be doing something else). She hopes to someday finish writing and illustrating her book, learn how to become invisible, and have an entire room full of tarantulas. View the online portfolio at www.dreamsoverzero.com.*

Holistic Sleep Magic

Tess Whitehurst

Getting a good night's sleep is a common magical intention. Many a spell has been cast, charm assembled, and potion brewed for that intention alone. But as it turns out, when it comes to manifesting, there's possibly nothing more powerful than the magical intention to regularly get a good night's sleep.

It sounds like I'm exaggerating, I know. But there is a good amount of data on the subject these days (see the recommended reading at the end of this article), and it's sparkly clear and reliably consistent: People who get more high-quality sleep actually (on average) make more money. They also (on average) live longer, have better relationships, are happier, are more creative, maintain a healthier weight, learn faster, solve problems more effectively, and are less likely to experience a car accident, have a mental illness, and or be diagnosed with cancer and other debilitating diseases like Alzheimer's and diabetes. What's more, recent studies have convincingly illustrated that our dreams are an essential aspect of processing and purifying ourselves of painful feelings and the emotional residue of past trauma.

In short, every aspect of your mind, body, and spirit—in order to be hearty and whole—absolutely requires the profound renewal that takes place during a healthy sleep cycle.

Truly, when you work magic for a good night's sleep—or take any other action that will help achieve this aim—every single aspect of your life experience will be blessed with staggering benefits. It follows that if you aren't getting a good night's sleep on a relatively consistent basis, there's no magical aim that would make more sense for you to prioritize.

Let's explore the art and science of getting a good night's sleep from a number of angles, and from both a practical and a magical standpoint.

What *Is* a Good Night's Sleep?

Before we explore what a good night's sleep actually is, let's begin with what it's not. First, it's *not* a prescription-induced stupor. According to neuroscientist Matthew Walker, in his book *Why We Sleep: Unlocking the Power of Sleep and Dreams*, sleep medications such as Ambien and Lunesta "do not provide natural sleep, can damage health, and increase the risk of life-threatening diseases" (Walker 2017, 282). In fact, he explains, they set up a vicious cycle that first drains sleep of many of its

most vital benefits, then requires patients to revive themselves during the day with caffeine, which then makes it even harder to fall asleep the following night, requiring even more of the drug to fall asleep. With this in mind, it should come as no surprise that with prolonged use of sleeping pills, the risks and challenges associated with them (including cancer and car accidents) continue to climb.

Similarly, while a drink or two before bed might *seem* to bless us with what we might describe as "a good night's sleep," regularly drinking alcohol actually robs our sleep of many of its most important functions, including support of short- and long-term memory as well as the emotionally healing, mentally balancing, and intelligence-boosting benefits of dreams. (Please don't panic if you currently rely on sleeping pills or alcohol to get to sleep. Instead, read on and learn some of the most powerful organic strategies for changing your relationship to sleep.)

What an ideal night in bed *will* entail is simple: seven to nine hours of natural slumber, unhindered by overuse of stimulants (such as caffeine) and minimally interrupted by waking for any reason.

What an ideal night in bed *will* entail is simple: seven to nine hours of natural slumber, unhindered by overuse of stimulants (such as caffeine) and minimally interrupted by waking for any reason.

Your Sacred Sleep Space

Considering the multifaceted power of sleep, it is certainly appropriate to think of sleep as sacred. You can therefore consider your bedroom a sacred space. Additionally, creating an optimal bedroom environment for sleep is the perfect starting point for your holistic sleep-magic efforts.

First, it's ideal to make simple and calming design choices in your bedroom. Loud, excessive, or overly ornate décor, as well as storage, electronics, exercise equipment, an overabundance of reading material, or clutter of any kind, will distract you and provide challenges to resting and relaxing deeply. And if you can avoid storing anything under the bed, you will likely find that it creates a much more positive, restful, and sleep-promoting ambience.

Too many mirrors in the bedroom can cause sleep disturbances, as the movement and light they reflect can be both energizing and unsettling. LED lights also create a significant challenge, as they trick our brain into thinking it's still daylight and therefore discourage us from properly winding down. Chose ambient lighting and keep it on the dimmer side, especially after sunset.

Obviously, a comfortable bed and pillow are essential. Keep in mind that solid-colored bedding is more restful to the eyes and mind than bedding that features patterns or prints. Remember, too, that imagery is powerful: when decorating the bedroom, only choose images that cause you to feel calm, restful, and serene.

On the metaphysical side of things, be sure to keep the energy in your bedroom cleansed and purified. Clean, dust, and vacuum (or sweep) at least once a week and follow up by smudging with a bundle of dried white sage, a stick of palo santo, or an aromatherapy or smudge spray of your choice. (Lavender, cedar, and sage are all good ingredient choices.) If you'd like, before bed each night, you can anoint your pillow with a calming essential oil, such as lavender or chamomile. You might find that keeping a black tourmaline under your pillow, on your nightstand, or in your hand while you sleep promotes a sense of safety, spiritual protection, and deep relaxation.

Vital Sleep Habits

Here are some simple, science-based habits that support deep, restful, and healing sleep.

Limit Screen Viewing

Computer, tablet, digital television, and smartphone screens—particularly when viewed during the hours before bed—are some of the most insidious sleep enemies in our modern world. That's why it's a good idea to limit computer and cell phone use before bed. Luckily, for the times when you still feel the need to look at a screen in the evening hours (like when you're watching TV while winding down after work), you can wear blue light-blocking glasses (available online) and program your phone and tablet to emit a more orange glow after sunset. (On iPhones, it's called "Night Shift.")

Cut Back on Caffeine

Coffee and tea (and other caffeine sources), as adored as they are by so many of us, can also pose a challenge to a good night's sleep. Much like sleeping pills giving us what *seems* like a good night's sleep (but isn't), caffeine seems to wake us up but actually just blocks the tiredness receptors in our brain and ramps up our stress hormones to whip us into action. While many sleep experts understandably recommend abstaining from caffeine altogether, simply cutting back can make a huge difference in how deeply you sleep. When you're used to letting the caffeine flow, I know cutting back sounds like no fun. I know because I've been there. When I became aware of the dire importance of deep sleep, however, here's what I did. First, I changed my morning cup of coffee to a cup of yerba mate. Then I switched my midday cup of black tea to a cup of green tea. Then I stopped drinking any caffeine at all after 11:30 a.m. At first, every incremental change was painful to some extent. But right away, my sleep deepened. And within just a few weeks, my natural energy returned. Not only that, but my moods were more sustainably positive, my energy was steadier and lasted longer (because it was fueled by sleep instead of caffeine), and my digestion was way more comfortable. Maybe one of these days I'll cut back even more, especially now that I know my natural energy will come back.

Satisfying substitutes I've found for caffeinated hot beverages include rooibos (or red) tea, tea containing reishi mushroom, and golden milk (a powdered mix containing turmeric that can be added to milk or milk substitutes). Energizing substitutes for iced caffeinated beverages include hibiscus tea, almond milk blended with maca and cacao (and sweetened with stevia and/or maple syrup), and sparkling water containing a tablespoon of apple cider vinegar.

EXERCISE

As if exercise didn't already have enough benefits, it also helps you sleep! (Conversely, the better sleep you get, the easier it becomes to motivate yourself to exercise, and to get in a good workout once you do.) You don't have to go crazy. As little as thirty minutes of moderate exercise five times a week is one of the most natural and reliable ways to coax your body into getting a full night of rest. Not to mention, a regular exercise habit—like sleep—bolsters your energy field and brings clarity to the mind, both of which supercharge your magical power.

WIND DOWN

So many of us go hard all day—right up until it's time for bed. And then we wonder why we can't get to sleep! Of course, our minds and bodies aren't light switches: they need a little time to slowly fade before shutting off for the night. So be sure to take a load off for at least an hour or two before it's time for bed. Perhaps meditate, read, spend time with your family, watch a show or two (with your blue light-blocking glasses, of course), or sit on the patio with a cup of chamomile tea. Extra credit if you have time for a hot bath!

Eat a Protein-Rich Diet

Recent studies indicate that when your diet is rich in protein, especially when you have a good bit of protein with your last meal of the day, you'll have an easier time falling asleep, and getting good-quality sleep once you do. Be sure not to eat too much of anything too close to bedtime though, as indigestion can interfere with your sleep. By the time bedtime rolls around, it's best if you can achieve a healthy balance of feeling satiated but not overly full.

Keep Your Feet Warm and Your Body Cool

Our brain gets the message that it's time to sleep only when our body temperature cools slightly. That's why the latest research indicates that a bedroom set at 65 degrees is ideal. It's also a good idea not to bundle up too much or swaddle yourself in excessive covers. On the other hand, warm feet support the biological conditions ideal for sleep. So keep it cool, but wear warm socks if needed.

Practice Good Sleep Hygiene

When you're establishing the habit of getting enough sleep, perhaps the most important tip of all is to practice good sleep hygiene. This means getting to bed and waking up at roughly (or precisely!) the same time almost every night, and giving yourself an eight- to nine-hour window of sleep opportunity. Regular timing supports your body's circadian rhythm, so you naturally wind down, sleep, and awake refreshed as a matter of course. Allowing a consistently ample window of time (even if you don't actually sleep the whole time every night) keeps you in the habit of respecting your sleep schedule, so you don't start to overbook your schedule and rob yourself of sleep's rejuvenating and life-enhancing benefits.

A New Perspective on Dream Magic

In his book *Why We Sleep*, Matthew Walker describes several studies that conclusively illustrate the multifaceted functions of dreams. First, our dreams contain emotions that we are processing and help us to purify ourselves of their painful residue. Second, our dreams synthesize what we've learned during the day and are a vital component of mastering complex things such as career skills, sports, and languages. Third, our dreams are laboratories of creativity. For example, Paul McCartney reportedly wrote his masterworks "Let It Be" and "Yesterday" after waking up from dreams about them.

Considering the fact that dreams help us purify ourselves of painful emotions, our feelings about nightmares bear reexamining. While some spells (perhaps even some I have written) are performed to "banish nightmares," maybe what we would benefit from focusing on instead is examining and processing the emotions they're mirroring so we can heal deeply and let go of any painful thoughts, memories, or beliefs we no longer need. In fact, it might even benefit us to be grateful for nightmares, as they are a free and natural form of therapy, showing us something deep within us that we are ready to release.

> **It might even benefit us to be grateful for nightmares, as they are a free and natural form of therapy, showing us something deep within us that we are ready to release.**

Furthermore, knowing that dreams support learning and mastering new skills, we can consciously employ them for that purpose during intense learning periods. I, for example, once waited tables at a Mexican restaurant. When I was learning the ropes, I remember bemoaning the fact that I would come home from waiting tables only to dream all night of filling baskets with tortilla chips and delivering hot plates covered in melted cheese. What I didn't realize at the time was that my dreams were streamlining the learning process and making it easier for me to get up to speed. If I knew then what I know now, I might have empowered a crystal before bed with the intention to sleep deeply, dream of my waitressing duties, and awake with great waitressing prowess, ready to enjoy a fun and prosperous day at work.

> **While science recognizes that dreams support creativity, those of us who are spiritually oriented might also suspect that the divine speaks to us and gifts us with inspiration while we sleep.**

While science recognizes that dreams support creativity, those of us who are spiritually oriented might also suspect that the divine speaks to us and gifts us with inspiration while we sleep. We are, after all, one with All That Is. So it's not much of a stretch to imagine that when our ego takes a holiday during our sleep, aspects of our true divine consciousness can saunter on into our psyche. (And I mean, have you *heard* those Paul McCartney songs?) As such, you might like to set the magical intention before bed to open up to a divine download while you sleep. Be sure to have a notebook, sketchbook, or recorder near your bed so you can document what you receive upon awakening.

CRYSTALS AND HERBS

A number of crystals and herbs can support deep and rejuvenating slumber with no negative side effects whatsoever. Here are some of my favorites.

Crystals

As I mentioned earlier, **black tourmaline** can promote a feeling of deep relaxation by cocooning us in a sense of energetic safety.

Many people enjoy keeping an **amethyst** under their pillow or on their nightstand to support harmonious and helpful dreams.

Kunzite is a good choice for those of us in the midst of heartache, grief, or unhealed emotional pain. It can help soften, open, and heal the heart while we sleep, and give us an increased ability to connect with others in a healthy way when we awaken.

Herbs

Hops, skullcap, valerian, passionflower, and chamomile are relaxing to the body and mind, and can be taken before bed alone or in combination as a tincture or herbal tea.

Kava reduces stress and relaxes the body and can be taken intermittently (not every night, as it can pose a challenge to the liver) to help you wind down, fall asleep, and sleep deeply.

Lavender essential oil can be applied directly to your pillowcase just before bed to promote deep and restful sleep. The dried blossoms are also a lovely addition to bedtime tea.

SLEEP-FRIENDLY DEITIES

In case you feel inspired to work with a deity or two for magical sleep support, here are some ideas.

Chandra, whose name means "moon," is the Hindu god of all things lunar. Light for him a white candle and a stick of lotus incense and request his support with learning astrology or other sacred metaphysical arts in your dreams. (Be sure to extinguish them before bed, though. No drifting off mid-invocation!)

Hygeia, while not specifically a sleep deity, has a vested interest in our sleep due to her identity as the Greek goddess of health, healing, and immunity. As such, she can help you establish and maintain healthy sleep habits and support you in experiencing restful and health-promoting sleep. Consider creating a simple altar to her in your bedroom, requesting her assistance and offering her a sleep-promoting herb (such as one or more of the herbs just mentioned) in a small bowl.

Morpheus is the Greek god of dreams. Offer him some poppy seeds or fresh poppies and request his support with any sort of dream-related intention, including healing old emotional pain, supporting the learning process, and receiving divine inspiration and insights.

Somnus is the Roman god of sleep. In fact, the roots of the word *insomniac* indicate a person without his blessing. As such, he's an excellent spirit to call on if you've been suffering from insomnia. Call on him after dark, under a dark moon, and offer him a freshly brewed cup of chamomile tea. Then request his assistance with getting to sleep.

Have Fun!

One of my favorite things about the magical path is that it transforms chores into projects and monotony into enchantment. So if you're inspired to change your sleep habits for the better, have fun with it! Call on a deity, blend up an herbal brew, and make a project out of arranging your sacred sleep space. Your body, mind, and spirit will thank you, and everything in your life will become infused with greater ease, harmony, clarity, energy, and delight.

Further Reading

Huffington, Arianna. *The Sleep Revolution: Transforming Your Life, One Night at a Time.* New York: Harmony Books, 2016.

Illes, Judika. *Encyclopedia of Spirits: The Ultimate Guide to the Magic of Fairies, Genies, Demons, Ghosts, Gods & Goddesses.* New York: HarperOne, 2009.

Walker, Matthew, PhD. *Why We Sleep: Unlocking the Power of Sleep and Dreams.* New York: Scribner, 2017.

Tess Whitehurst *teaches magical and intuitive arts in live workshops and via her online community and learning hub,* The Good Vibe Tribe Online School of Magical Arts. *An award-winning author, she's written eight books, which have been translated into eighteen languages. She's appeared on Bravo, Fox, and NBC, and her writing has been featured in* Writer's Digest *and* Spirit & Destiny *(in the UK) and on her popular website, tesswhitehurst.com.*

So You Had a Bad Day: Magickal Stress Tamers

Monica Crosson

I'm at my happiest when I'm in my garden tugging at weeds, watching honey bees flit from blossom to blossom, and listening to the caws of crows who nest in the trees surrounding my home. It is from my garden that I gather herbs for spells, teas, and tinctures and pick the berries that will be made into jam so we may be reminded of summer's sweetness throughout the winter to come. As I putter around my greenhouse, the scent of tomatoes and rich humus takes me back to days spent in my grandmother's greenhouse, gleaning from her everything I know about organic gardening. One of my favorite meditation spots is under a weeping willow that graces the edge of my garden and whose branches hang in leafy curtains—a protective wall of green.

But the truth of the matter is that I don't always get to be in my garden flouncing around blissfully in a floral skirt or creating tea blends or meditating under a favorite tree. My life isn't a fairy tale, and I face stress in one form or another all the time. And some days can be particularly bad. We've all had those days where life throws us one small humiliation after another, and we are left stressed-out and wanting to curl into the fetal position in the corner of our bedroom. Stress is something that for most of us cannot be avoided and, if not kept in check, can adversely affect our health. Problems such as high blood pressure, diabetes, heart disease, and obesity may all be exacerbated by stress.

Stress affects us all differently, so what can be a bad day for me might be not be for you. As a true Cancerian, I have a tendency to want to please everyone and can lie sleepless for hours worrying about whether or not I hurt someone's feelings, but that might not be something that you struggle with. On the other hand, you might be stressed about having to write a research paper or overseeing the ritual for your circle's next sabbat celebration, and I'm like, "Bring it on!"

I don't always get to be in my garden flouncing around blissfully in a floral skirt or creating tea blends or meditating under a favorite tree. My life isn't a fairy tale, and I face stress in one form or another all the time.

Though we can't stop bad days from happening, there are a few tricks that might lessen the stress that accompanies them when the universe gives us a kick in the pants.

Mercury Retrograde Tips

Besides the stresses we face in our everyday mundane lives, I find that many of my magickal friends get a little added dose of anxiety approximately three times per year. Yes, I'm talking about Mercury retrograde! I don't know about you, but for me, the few weeks while Mercury appears to backtrack through the sky is basically one long bad day. I often feel physically sluggish, with a tendency toward self-degradation. My typically patient attitude dissolves and I become easily agitated, with little or no provocation. And while I am a highly intuitive individual, and though my intuitive nature remains intact, during a Mercury retrograde my chest tightens and I sometimes get nervous before something happens.

Don't be surprised if your stress level increases when Mercury is retrograde. Remember, Mercury rules communication, and that includes learning, reading, speaking, listening, buying, selling and any other type of negotiation. Mercury also rules over travel, technology, and media. As I write this (during a Mercury retrograde), I am dealing with a brand-new printer that is jammed with a tiny piece of paper that I cannot get out, and I think it will cost more to pay for someone to fix it than to buy a new one (takes deep cleansing breath).

To deal with the added stress of a Mercury retrograde, the best thing you can do for yourself is just to be aware of what's going on. Mark these periods on your calendar and remind yourself that Mercury will eventually go direct once again. Here are a few other simple ways to avoid stress during a Mercury retrograde.

Avoid Change

Use this time for reflection. Try journaling or revisiting an old hobby or abandoned project. Avoid beginning new endeavors or making drastic changes.

Clear Communication

Acknowledge the possibility of miscommunication during this time, and don't kick yourself too hard if your foot does happen to go into your mouth. Remember to take time to process the situation, and avoid debates and important conversations with friends, family, or coworkers. Take time to listen.

Manage your Schedule

This isn't the time to be spontaneous. If possible, avoid planning trips during a Mercury retrograde (unless you're doing something you've done before), and make use of that empty planner.

Stay Calm

Mercury retrograde doesn't affect everyone the same way. Just be aware of the subtle (or not so subtle) influences it has on you and remind yourself that it's a temporary situation that will pass.

Take a Nature Bath

As a magickal practitioner, I know the value of being outdoors. It helps slow me down after a long, strenuous day and reminds me that I am truly a part of the weave of nature. Researchers in Japan conducted experiments in which they measured the cortisol level, heart rate, blood pressure, and pulse of volunteers before and after a walk (Park et al. 2010). Part of the group walked through the forest, while the other walked through the city. What they found was not surprising. In test after test, they found that a walk through the forest lowered blood pressure, heart rate, parasympathetic nerve activity, and cortisol levels. In another study, researchers found that the presence of essential oils released from trees (phytoncides) appeared to boost the immune system (Li et al. 2008). So if just a walk does that, think of all that can be gained by literally bathing yourself in nature!

Nature bathing is not really bathing at all. It's taking the time to absorb the positive vibrations that come with being in nature.

Lie beneath your favorite tree. How does the cool grass feel on your back and arms? Enjoy the meditative sway of the branches above you. Listen to the sound of the breeze as it moves the leaves and the sound of birds chirping from their nests.

You don't have to restrict nature bathing to the forest. If you're more of a Sea Witch, remember to take your shoes off and sink your toes into the sand. Lay your head back and feel the heat of the sun as it plays across your skin. Allow yourself to be lulled into a meditative state by the sound of the waves lapping on the shore.

Nature bathing is not really bathing at all. It's taking the time to absorb the positive vibrations that come with being in nature.

Try bathing in your favorite natural setting for at least fifteen minutes a few times a week and see if it makes a difference.

Stones That Alleviate Stress

Stones and crystals are great tools that can help promote physical, emotional, and spiritual healing. Here are a few of my favorites for stress relief.

AMETHYST

This is great for stress relief and also improves clarity and focus.

BLACK TOURMALINE

This protective stone is great for warding off negative vibes and transmuting them into positive energy.

BLUE LACE AGATE

This tranquil blue stone brings on a sense of peace and promotes loving energy.

BLUE SODALITE

This stone for peace has a comforting energy that helps stimulate self-confidence.

CARNELIAN

This energy-boosting stone increases confidence and inspiration.

CLEAR CRYSTAL

This stone resonates with your higher chakra levels and is emotionally and spiritually healing.

HIMALAYAN SALT

This is calming and eases emotional stress. You may already have a Himalayan salt lamp near your bed or on a shelf and are aware of its ability to release negative ions into the room to create a more relaxing environment. Try using salt crystals in your bath to wash away anxiety.

MOONSTONE

Believed to balance female hormones, this stone may also relieve stress, heighten intuition, and stabilize emotions.

ROSE QUARTZ

This is a classic stone for love and harmony. Carry it on you for peace and tranquility.

"This Too Shall Pass" Charm Bag

Whenever my family faced a stressful situation, my mom always said, "Remember, honey, this too shall pass." So whether it's a doctor appointment or a dreaded dinner party, carry this small charm bag with you as a reminder that very few things in life are permanent.

Gather the following items:

- A small drawstring pouch

- A small rose quartz crystal

- ½ teaspoon lavender buds

- ¼ teaspoon bee balm

- A small personal object that gives you comfort (such as a button, coin, or other memento)

Place the ingredients in the pouch one at a time, focusing on peace and harmony. Tie three knots in the drawstring. As you tie each one, say, "And this too shall pass."

Essential Oils to Alleviate Stress

When inhaled, essential oils can help stimulate the limbic system (the part of your brain that influences your emotions and motivation). Here are a few essential oils that may help lessen the effects of stress.

BERGAMOT

With its uplifting and refreshing scent, this oil gives you a boost of energy.

CHAMOMILE

This calming oil soothes anxious feelings.

CLARY SAGE

Clary sage is known to have a positive influence on dopamine levels, so its uplifting scent can relieve anxiety symptoms.

LAVENDER

This is the most commonly used oil to relieve stress, and for good reason—its pleasing scent is relaxing and can improve focus.

LEMONGRASS

This brightly scented oil promotes relaxation and relieves anxious feelings.

MARJORAM

This calming oil alleviates anxious feelings and helps soothe grief.

PEPPERMINT

This oil helps to keep you alert and alleviates mental fatigue.

YLANG-YLANG

This oil helps to relieve anger-induced stress.

Stress Buster Essential Oil Blend

Create your own stress-taming essential oil blend that you can use whenever anxious feelings begin to surface.

You will need the following:

• A 2-ounce glass bottle of your choice (with lid)

• 8 teaspoons carrier oil (Fractionated coconut oil and grapeseed oil are my favorites.)

• 5 drops lavender essential oil

• 2 drops chamomile essential oil

• 2 drops bergamot essential oil

Mix the oils together and pour into the bottle. Use a drop on each temple and on pulse points as needed.

Dream Away Anxiety

Herbal pillows have been used for centuries to induce peaceful sleep, enhance dreams, encourage dream memory, and protect against nightmares. No matter the reason, herbal pillows are beneficial for everyone.

> **Herbal pillows have been used for centuries to induce peaceful sleep, enhance dreams, encourage dream memory, and protect against nightmares.**

To prepare an herbal pillow, select a piece of fabric, preferably a piece of cotton or another natural fiber. Wash and dry the fabric. Don't use scented detergent or fabric softener—it will take away from your herbal mix. Now cut the fabric into whatever shape you wish. Squares and rectangles are the easiest to cut, but go ahead and get creative. Moon and star shapes are fun and relatively easy to make.

Next, create a blend of sleep-inducing herbs using one of the mixes I suggest in the next section, or craft your own mixture with fragrant herbs you find pleasing. With the right sides of the fabric together, stitch along the edges, leaving a ¼-inch seam allowance and making sure to leave an open space along one side. When you've finished stitching, flip the pillow out through the open space and fill with your herbal blend. Finish the pillow by hand-stitching the opening shut. You may add embellishments such as buttons, lace, or embroidery. Be creative!

Herbs to Encourage Restful Sleep

Sleep pillows are great for anyone who has difficulty falling asleep. To create a blend that supports a deep, peaceful sleep, combine any of the following herbs:

Balsam fir needles: Relaxing, soothing

Catnip: Relaxing; helps bring deep sleep

Chamomile: Calming, relaxing; keeps bad dreams away

Cinquefoil: For a restful sleep or to dream of a new lover

Hops: Relaxing; brings peacefulness

Lavender: Soothing, relaxing; induces sleep and relieves headaches

Lemon balm: Eases stress, anxiousness, and nervousness; good for insomnia and headaches

Linden: Promotes sleep

Marjoram: Calms restlessness and nervousness

Rose petals: Brings warmth and love

Rosemary: Encourages a deep, restful sleep and keeps away bad dreams

Thyme: Ensures pleasant sleep and drives away nightmares

Stress-Tamer Herb Blend

This blend works well to take the edge off a stressful day.

½ cup hops

½ cup mugwort

⅛ cup sweet marjoram

Out Like a Light Herb Blend

This blend promotes deep, restful sleep.

½ cup lavender

¼ cup hops

¼ cup mugwort

. . . .

When you're going through a tough time, remember that stress management should always include a healthy diet, regular exercise, meditation, and a little time set aside for whatever makes you happy—whether it be reading a good book in a cozy chair or spending a little time in your own magickal garden. Tend to the needs of your soul for a happier, more magickal you!

Source List

Li, Q., K. Morimoto, et al. "A Forest Bathing Trip Increases Human Natural Killer Activity and Expression of Anti-Cancer Proteins in Female Subjects." *Journal of Biological Regulators and Homeostatic Agents* 22, no. 1 (January–March 2008): 45–55.

Park, B. J., Y. Tsunetsugu, et al. "The Physiological Effects of Shinrin-Yoku (Taking In the Forest Atmosphere or Forest Bathing): Evidence from Field Experiments in 24 Forests across Japan." *Environmental Health and Preventive Medicine* 15, no. 1 (January 2010): 18–26.

Monica Crosson *is a Master Gardener who lives in the beautiful Pacific Northwest, happily digging in the dirt and tending to her raspberries with her family and a menagerie of adopted animals. She has been a practicing Witch for over twenty-five years and is a member of Blue Moon Coven. Monica is the author of* The Magickal Family: Pagan Living in Harmony with Nature, *released by Llewellyn in 2017.*

The Relief of Winter: Magick to Lighten and Brighten the Cold Winter Days

Najah Lightfoot

I'm sitting down to write this article during the hottest time of year. When I awoke this morning, before I could even think about getting my thoughts on the page, I was sweaty and hot. My nightclothes were sticking to me and I was annoyed that the cool of our basement bedroom wasn't enough to break the heat of a summer night.

I live in Denver, Colorado. As a city dweller, I've learned that if you manage to get up early, you can catch the cool breezes of the morning before the blistering temperatures of a mile-high summer day settle upon you.

Rising early on summer mornings also brings the benefit of quiet time. If you get up early, you can experience the still, precious moments of a new day before every car or bus gets going or a construction crew starts pounding away with jackhammers.

I like to call these quiet times of the dawn my "Zen moments." I love these moments that allow me to be outside, saying my prayers and performing my daily ritual of giving thanks and gratitude. I love this time of the morning when I can be alone in my own little world, listening to birds, gazing at trees, and watching clouds light up with the first rays of the morning sun.

When I am alone during these Zen moments, I can think. I can take time to patiently look at my flowers and water my plants. I enjoy doing these things in the quiet hours of the morning before the heat of a summer day comes blasting down upon me.

When I'm hot and sweaty, it doesn't take much for my mind to turn to thoughts of a snowy, cold winter. It's as if we're never satisfied. When we're hot, we want to be cold. When we're cold, we want to be hot. And with climate change rearing its ugly head, the hot seems to be getting hotter and the cold seems to be getting more brutal, bone-chilling, and downright miserable.

But as I sit in the present moment writing this article during the dog days of summer, it will be several months before the relief of winter sets in. Autumn still needs to arrive, and when the days do turn chilly and the early snows begin to fall in the Northern Hemisphere, the holiday schedule will blast into full swing and we'll all be running around like mad squirrels, dashing here, there, and everywhere. As the seasons change and Northern Hemisphere dwellers prepare for cold temps and long nights, our co-Earth dwellers in the Southern Hemisphere will be getting ready to put on shorts and flip-flops and head to the beach or start working in their gardens. No one escapes the turn of the Wheel.

During the months of October, November, and December, there will be holiday parties, rituals, and celebrations to attend. We will have gifts to buy, costumes to wear, and cards to write and send. Some will use the avenue of online shopping to get their items off and running, while others will use good old-fashioned postage stamps and wait in line at the post office. Whatever avenue we choose, for many of us it will seem like an endless, exhausting, mad parade of do, do, do and do some more. Even the most stoic of us won't be able to escape the commercialism, the socialism, and, for some dear ones, the depression or sad memories the holiday season can bring.

And then suddenly, as if someone flipped a light switch, the month of January will arrive and everything will go quiet.

The festive trees, lights, and baubles will come down. We won't have any more days or long weekends off from work. The letdown from all the parties and get-togethers will set in, and winter and the north wind will truly arrive in all their glory.

The earth will appear to have gone quiet and dormant. There will be no more flowers or leaves on the trees. The ground will be hard as a rock, and in some places covered in a blanket of pristine snow. If you get up early and fresh snow has fallen, you may catch magical ice crystals sparkling in the morning sun. As your bones chill and you lug around what seems like forty pounds of clothing on your body to stay to warm, your thoughts and endless commercials will tease your mind with images of warm, sunny beaches, balmy summer days, and nights spent outdoors on the veranda.

But wait. Weren't you just longing for winter a few short months ago? Wasn't it you lamenting how hot and miserable you were, and how you couldn't wait for winter to arrive?

It can be difficult to stay in the present moment. It seems we're never able to stay in the *now*. We're constantly looking ahead or planning for a date in the far-off, distant future.

Thankfully, Mother Nature is wise and knows better than we do. She gifts us with winter, which can force us to hunker down, stay inside, and reflect and contemplate.

Thankfully, Mother Nature is wise and knows better than we do. She gifts us with winter, which can force us to hunker down, stay inside, and contemplate. Winter forces us to turn within.

Cold, chilly, can't-go-outside days force us to pause and look around. As we look at nature in her winter state, we may assume the trees are dead as they stand tall and stark naked against the cold and ice. We know they aren't really dead, even though they look that way. We know they are storing sap, feeding their roots, and gathering earth energy until fresh buds and new growth appear in the spring.

We know spring will return, because that is nature's promise. After winter, spring always returns. Such is the nature of life.

Magickal Winter Crafts

While you're trudging around in the snow or stuck inside loathing the cold weather, how can you use the relief of winter to bring some magick into your life? You can get crafty and have some fun! You can use your witchy imagination and childlike sense of wonder to brighten up the cold and bring light to dreary days.

Plant Magick

A hot glue gun, some leftover trinkets, and inexpensive clay pots can entertain your magickal, childlike mind for hours. You can have fun gluing crystals, beads, or trinkets on the outside of clay pots. You may even choose to draw pictures on them, paint them whimsical colors, or fill them with crystals, faux plants, and flowers.

If your home is lucky enough to get bright sun during the winter, you could also plant some nice, hardy houseplants, such as ivy or winter cactus, in your pots. If your home doesn't get bright light during the winter, you can always buy a "day light" light bulb and place your potted plants in the light and enjoy watching them grow while winter rages all around you.

When spring arrives, if you have chosen to leave your pots empty while awaiting warmer temperatures, you can now fill them with potting soil and plants, which will brighten your home, yard, or office. If you placed plants in your pots during the winter, they will now be nice and healthy, and you may decide to keep them in their magickal pots all year long.

Either way, before spring arrives, while the north wind is blowing through you, you can look at your magickal pots and daydream. Your decorated pots can be a mystical nudge for your intuition and creative mind to ponder the things you will grow, or the places you will go, when the days become warm again.

Coloring Books

Consider purchasing some magickal coloring books. Coloring books for adults are all the rage now, and some of us never stopped coloring. A winter's-day field trip to the art store will provide you with loads of choices. There are coloring books of mandalas, prisms, flowers, Celtic imagery, and tattoo art, just to name a few. You can also purchase nifty colored markers at an art store and use them as your magickal coloring wands. When you arrive home from your field trip, make your favorite hot drink, burn a little incense, put on some good music, and have yourself a coloring fiesta!

PUZZLES

Puzzles are a wonderful way to bring the family together and enjoy doing something that is good for the mind and spirit. Another nice thing about puzzles is they don't need to be finished all at once, which makes them a great choice to while away winter hours.

Find a space or table you can designate for puzzle fun. You may even choose to cover the space with a bright cloth that fuels your imagination and creativity. Pick a puzzle with a theme of fun and intriguing images. As the days of winter slowly go by, you can sit at your puzzle for as long or as little you like, adding piece after piece until you finally achieve your goal of a finished piece of art. If you find yourself becoming attached to the image as it begins to take shape, once your puzzle is finished, you can buy puzzle glue at the craft store, glue all the pieces together, and have a cherished keepsake of how you spent your winter!

. . . .

The dull days of winter need not be ones to abhor or simply trudge through. You can find magick in the quiet. Allow your imagination and sense of wonder to take you into the realm of sparkly ice crystals and have some fun. Who knows? Now that you are armed with magickal crafts and tools for cold winter days, winter may just become your favorite season.

Najah Lightfoot *is an initiated member of La Source Ancienne Ounfo, a sister-priestess of the Divine Feminine, and an active member of the Denver Pagan community. She keeps her magick strong through the practice of Kung Fu, the folk magick of Hoodoo, Pagan rituals, and her belief in the mysteries of the universe. She finds inspiration in movies, music, and the blue skies of Colorado. Find her online at www.twitter.com/NajahLightfoot, www.facebook.com/NajahLightfoot, www.instagram.com/NajahLightfoot, and www.craftandconjure.com.*

Transforming Trauma

Dallas Jennifer Cobb

I live with complex PTSD as a result of excessive childhood trauma and the subsequent pattern of retraumatization carried through my early adult years. While living with and healing my complex PTSD (post-traumatic stress disorder), I have used many magical techniques to transform trauma. This is not an easy practice. It really is the hardest and most meaningful magical work that I do—transforming trauma into resilience.

Statistics show that trauma is widespread and has many sources, and many North Americans have experienced trauma. With new neurological and psychological research contributing to the field, I have found a few techniques that have enabled me to break the cycle of retraumatization, reduce the number and severity of flashbacks, identify and limit retraumatizing behavior, and create structures and routines that enable me to dwell more in the present. Let me share some simple and easy-to-learn techniques with you so that you too can transform trauma.

I have used many magical techniques to transform trauma. This is not an easy practice. It really is the hardest and most meaningful magical work that I do.

What Is Trauma and PTSD?

The Oxford Dictionary defines *trauma* as a deeply distressing or disturbing experience or physical injury.

Post-traumatic stress disorder is described as a severe response to trauma, and it is most powerfully characterized by three prominent symptoms (Wolkin 2016):

1. Reexperiencing the event

2. Avoiding any reminders of the event or feeling emotionally numb

3. Hyper-arousal, which consists of a very sensitive startle response

It has been shown that when the brain is experiencing PTSD, it can get caught up in a highly alert state that is constantly activated and perceives threats everywhere. Reliving their trauma over and over again, survivors often resort to "fight, flight, freeze, or fawn" mode as they withdraw from the present and reinhabit the traumatic past.

How Prevalent Is Trauma?

The Sidran Institute's "Post Traumatic Stress Disorder Fact Sheet" estimates that approximately 70 percent of adults in the United States have experienced a traumatic event in their lives, and 20 percent of that group develop PTSD. It is estimated that more than 13 million Americans suffer from PTSD at this time. But sadly, this statistic excludes children and teens.

A recent study conducted by Dr. Robert Anda on behalf of the Centers for Disease Control and Prevention indicates that adverse childhood experiences are the largest widespread health issue that the United States now faces. The study attempted to document the number of children and teens affected by sexual, emotional, and physical abuse, emotional and physical neglect, exposure to substance abuse, domestic violence, divorce or separation, household mental illness, or incarceration. The findings were staggering. The sheer number of simple and complex traumatic experiences faced by children and teens indicates that the actual number of people experiencing trauma in the United States is much higher than estimated.

The secondary risks associated with trauma include an increased probability of smoking, alcohol and drug abuse, promiscuity, and severe obesity, and correlate with health issues including depression, heart disease, cancer, and a shortened lifespan—issues that carry with them a high price tag for the provision of legal, institutional, health, and mental health care for the survivors as children and as they age.

Trauma is a modern plague.

Transforming Trauma

Post-traumatic stress disorder was the definitive medical name assigned to the widespread occurrence and symptoms of psychological illness faced by survivors of trauma. PTSD is now entered into the DSM (Diagnostic and Statistical Manual of Mental Disorders).

After a lifetime spent treating trauma survivors and writing about the evolution in assessment, diagnosis, and treatment, Dr. Bessel van der Kolk, one of the world's foremost experts on trauma, became aware of the failings of psychiatry, talk therapy, and pharmacological intervention. It appeared that survivors were not getting better from just talk therapy, and the improvements made with pharmacological intervention were short-lived and drug-dependent. He found that veterans who were learning breathing and meditation techniques and yoga actually experienced greater transformation of their symptoms. This realization drove Van der Kolk in a new direction, and his current research focuses on using alternative methods in the treatment of trauma. By focusing on "soothing the brain," Van der Kolk found that anything that promoted feelings of peace, safety, and security increased brain serotonin levels, and increased the well-being and ability to cope socially for survivors of trauma (Van der Kolk 2014, 34).

> **Improvements made with pharmacological intervention were short-lived and drug-dependent…. Veterans who were learning breathing and meditation techniques and yoga actually experienced greater transformation of their symptoms.**

While improved diet, increased time outdoors, exercise, orgasm, healthy relationships, and good-quality sleep have been shown to greatly affect perceived levels of well-being and increase serotonin levels, Van der Kolk also studied the effects of EMDR (eye movement desensitization and reprocessing), meditation, yoga, mindfulness, relaxation, and visualization and found that all of these helped trauma survivors minimize the effects of trauma, transforming themselves through engaged peaceful embodiment.

It turns out that trauma and peace cannot coexist. Where fighting, suppressing, or talking about trauma only serves to keep the survivor in a traumatized state, finding ways to experience calm, peace, safety, security, and a sense of belonging all foster significant positive gains in the transformation of trauma. After years of twelve-step meetings, individual and group therapy, recovery from addiction, and ongoing retraumatization, I finally found relief from trauma through engaging in serotonin-inducing experiences and practices, including mindful magic, practiced alone and in community.

Trauma-Sensitive Magic

"Magic is the art of changing consciousness at will," Dion Fortune is credited as saying. So any tools that enable us to shift out of trauma and into a grounded and centered state of being are "magical" tools. Whether it is learning what triggers us and then knowing how to "reset" ourselves after being triggered, or using elemental tools to ground, center, protect, and bless, magic has a central place in the trauma-informed practice of living.

Developing tools to manage your own trauma is empowering, but taking those tools out into the community is a much harder practice. When planning our community rituals, my magical circle considers many aspects. Adopting a trauma-sensitive approach, we attempt to minimize possible triggers in our rituals. We avoid sudden, complete darkness, heavy incense, startling noises, and unexpected touching or hugging. We use trauma-informed techniques to ground and center participants, enabling them to feel present in the circle and aware of the space they are sharing with the people around them. We verbally remind people to both check in with their bodies and use movement to help them stay embodied. By incorporating these simple practices, we practice trauma-informed magic and promote it in our community.

Elemental Tools to Transform Trauma

I use a variety of elemental tools on a daily basis to help me transform trauma. Whether they possess finite physical health benefits, act on an energetic level, or engage me mentally, each element plays a role in helping to anchor me and maintain a solution-oriented focus. I am aware of the present moment and of transforming my conscience at will.

Experiment with a variety of elemental tools and see what works best for you. Gemstones and crystals, essential oils, and herbs are widely available in New Age and health-food stores or online.

HEALING GEMSTONES

Gemstones are handy because they can be made into jewelry and worn throughout the day. They are portable elemental tools that enable you to take their qualities with you wherever you go. Feel the need for protection? Wear amethyst on a chain around your neck. Concerned about negativity in the workplace? Let a chunk of black tourmaline absorb and purify the energy so you don't have to. Here are a few commonly used and widely available crystal gemstones and their energetic uses:

- **Amethyst** is used for protection, purification, and the healing of addictions.

- **Black tourmaline** provides purification and protection and can be used to absorb negativity.

- **Fluorite** helps to clear energy fields, enhances decision-making ability, and provides mental clarity.

- **Garnet** promotes emotional healing and improves your sense of security, strength, and self-worth.

- **Obsidian** can help you to shake off negativity, ground yourself, and invoke psychic protection.

- **Pink tourmaline** is known to promote emotional healing and anchor feelings of love.

- **Rose quartz** also helps with emotional healing and promotes gentleness and soft care.

- **Seraphinite** encourages self-healing, wholeness of spirit, and the regeneration of brain cells. It counters depression and promotes feelings of well-being, happiness, and calm.

HELPFUL ESSENTIAL OILS

When I was engaged in ongoing therapy, I regularly used lavender essential oil to soothe and calm my jangled nerves. Essential oils should be diluted with a carrier oil. I like almond or olive oil because they are richly moisturizing and feel luxurious. (If you have nut allergies, beware.)

Before leaving the sanctity of my home, I like to ritualistically apply diluted **lavender essential oil**, affirming, "I am safe, I am happy, I am healthy, I am peaceful." Through the repetition of affirmations and the physical anchoring in the present through scent, I feel more able to explore the troubling memories of and associations from the past in therapy. Sometimes all I need to do is to consciously inhale and settle my awareness on the scent of lavender, and just like that I feel calmer.

To promote feeling grounded, peaceful, and accepted, I often turn to earthy **patchouli essential oil**. This calming oil is often used in incenses for meditation because of its deeply peaceful energy. While applying patchouli, gaze at your feet and say, "I'm grounded." Place your palms together and affirm, "I'm at peace." Then place your hands over your heart and deeply feel your own acceptance. Intone, "I am that I am."

To promote clarity, energy, and focused attention, try **peppermint essential oil**, which has an awakening and enlivening quality. Peppermint is also used for cleansing and purification and relieves nausea. I often use peppermint oil in a diffuser in my home to keep it feeling fresh, alive, and awake. My home is my safe space, so making it feel lively and energized is important. During times when I slipped into depression and avoidance, my home started to smell sour, stale, and decaying. Let peppermint be both the prevention and the cure for what ails you.

Rose essential oil provides me with deep feelings of self-love and self-acceptance. Whenever I apply rose essential oil, I feel luxurious, rich, and royal. It reminds me to take gentle care of myself. Near my local library, there is a wild rose bush that produces the most fragrant flowers. I always take time to stop and smell the roses, literally. Each inhale of rose essential oil helps me cultivate deep feelings of specialness, self-worth, and self-love. Who needs roses from someone else when there is rose essential oil to remind us of the sacred practice of self-love?

> **Rose essential oil provides me with deep feelings of self-love and self-acceptance. Whenever I apply rose essential oil, I feel luxurious, rich, and royal.**

Rosemary essential oil is commonly used for purification and cleansing. It promotes peace and activates your self-healing capacity. Putting a couple drops of rosemary essential oil in the laundry, especially on sheets, pillowcases, and towels, helps me feel sacred and uplifted. The purification that comes through this scent is emotional, spiritual, and physical, enabling me to feel sanctified and anointed. Use it to restore your sacred space and sacred sense of self.

HERBS FOR MENTAL HEALTH

Here are a few versatile and easy-to-find herbs that really help to keep me in the present.

Lavender (*Lavandula angustifolia*) is something that I grow and dry for use year round. When my nerves get jangled, if I have been triggered and experience retraumatization, or if I have slept poorly and had nightmares, brewing a cup of lavender tea can help me feel soothed and calmed. Simply take two lavender florets, cover them with boiling water, and let brew for five minutes before drinking. For extra-sweet healing and soul balming, stir in a teaspoon of honey. Sip slowly and feel your internal landscape smooth over and become serene. With each sip, feel the warmth infuse you with a calm presence.

While **St. John's wort** (*Hypericum perforatum*) is widely known to help reduce the effects of depression, it has also been used historically as a protective talisman to ward off evil, protect against disease, and fortify magical powers (Hobbs). Whether you make a tincture or add some of the blossoms to an infusion, invoke the protection and strength of St. John's wort. I often imagine St. John as a scythe-wielding warrior taking on my depression and fighting down the demons from the past.

Valerian root (*Valeriana officinalis*) is something I have turned to at times when I have been plagued by nightmares, sleeplessness, and anxiety. It promotes deep sleep, easy dreams, and an uplifted spirit. Though it is good at offsetting depression, valerian is something I take only at night, because it really does make me tired and slow-moving. Invite valerian in to help you get the restorative sleep you need and the peaceful dreams you desire. Valerian also has an anti-anxiety effect.

Name It and Tame It

While trauma is the plague of this era, we Witches are healers. Use your magical practices individually, collectively, and in community to incorporate more and more trauma-sensitive practices. Make healing an everyday act.

Magic rituals can be used for the empowering act of naming and taming trauma and not just for the prevention of retraumatization. In the safety of my new moon circle, I started to shape ritual around the release of the secrets I had held since childhood. Through magical scribing and burning, chanting and singing, my circle has helped me name, tame, and release the shame, guilt, and toxicity I have carried as a result of childhood abuse.

Do not undertake this sort of magic lightly. The deep emotion of compacted and long-suppressed trauma can be volatile and unpredictable. Using elemental magic and ritual for the transformation of trauma is not suitable for those who are still deeply enmeshed in the circular pattern of being triggered and constantly replaying the past. Instead, help them find the trusted support they need to undertake the quiet practice of their early healing journey.

But those who are able to name and tame their demons can use ritual to empower and strengthen themselves. Emphasize the positive—invoke healing, practice protection, and cast circles of safety and inclusivity. These simple acts of collective caring have deep and far-reaching healing effects. They counteract trauma by drawing people into community, into belonging, and into love. Ultimately, the love of community that holds us tenderly is what most deeply transforms consciousness.

And that is powerfully transformative magic.

Resources

Anda, Robert. "Overview of the Adverse Childhood Experiences (ACE) Study." Centers for Disease Control and Prevention. Accessed Feb. 1, 2019. https://multco.us/file/37959/download.

Hobbs, Christopher. "St. John's Wort: Ancient Herbal Protector." Accessed Feb. 1, 2019. https://www.christopherhobbs.com/library /articles-on-herbs-and-health/st-johns-wort-ancient-herbal-protector/.

Sidran Institute. "Post Traumatic Stress Disorder Fact Sheet." Accessed Feb. 1, 2019. https://www.sidran.org/resources/for-survivors-and-loved -ones/post-traumatic-stress-disorder-fact-sheet-2/.

Van der Kolk, Bessel. *The Body Keeps the Score*. New York: Penguin, 2014.

Wolkin, Jennifer. "The Science of Trauma, Mindfulness, and PTSD." Mindful, June 15, 2016. https://www.mindful.org/the-science-of -trauma-mindfulness-ptsd/.

Dallas Jennifer Cobb *practices gratitude magic, giving thanks for ongoing healing, wholeness, and prosperity; a variety of flexible and rewarding work; and quiet contentment. She lives with her daughter in paradise: a waterfront village in rural Ontario, where she regularly swims, hikes, meditates, and snowshoes. A Reclaiming witch from way back, Jennifer is part of an eclectic pan-Pagan circle that organizes large magical and empowering community rituals. Contact her at jennifer.cobb@live.com.*

Rekindling a Witch: Confronting Turmoil and Emerging Empowered

Michael Furie

At some point, we all have "one of those days." You know, times when everything just seems to go wrong. This is a normal part of existence, but when "one of those years" rolls around, it can feel like a punch in the gut that is too difficult to overcome.

Not so long ago, my family suffered a sudden tragic loss that threw us all into chaos and despair. My family is rather small, and to lose someone without being able to say goodbye was a devastating blow. This had a domino effect that threatened to tear apart my very sense of self. As a Witch who embraces the natural cycles, celebrates the sabbats and seasons, and has stood on the threshold between life and death on more than one occasion, I have acknowledged, honored, and respected the different phases of growth and decline, life and death, for over two decades. Without realizing it, I had built up this subconscious idea that because I was so tuned in to the natural world, I would somehow have an edge against times of sorrow. The last couple years have been an intense education in the realities of grief and loss, as well as the balance of strength needed to make peace with the past and move into the future empowered and with a renewed purpose.

It's unfortunate that during times of strife, everything can seem so hollow. Things that used to bring a smile to my face were upsetting to me and felt frivolous. It felt wrong to laugh or feel even the smallest amount of joy lest I risk "forgetting what's really important."

In addition to restricting myself from feeling lighthearted joy, I found that my magical work also felt pointless. My thinking was that since I had been unsuccessful in healing my loved one, my magic was no longer effective.

In addition to restricting myself from feeling lighthearted joy, I found that my magical work also felt pointless. My thinking was that since I had been unsuccessful in healing my loved one, my magic was no longer effective. For several months I had convinced myself that my abilities were waning, and as such, bothering with ritual or spellwork seemed not only foolish but also an affront to the higher powers that had apparently left me in this state. I'd fallen so far that at that point I was angry and resentful of spirit and the divine. The hurt in my heart had taken such strong root that I felt as though the gods and ancestors had decided that I was no longer worthy of their attention, let alone their assistance.

Even writing, which up to that point had been my refuge, became a huge source of anxiety as I struggled to regain my inner strength. My writing is very personal, and I absolutely refused to merely form some semblance of "appropriate witchiness" in order to maintain the pace of my work. Instead, I seriously considered giving up writing altogether. As I sat for what seemed like endless hours in front of my computer, staring at the half paragraph I'd been able to type, desperately trying to muster up some kind of inspiration to keep going, I found it impossible to express what I needed to say.

As time went by and the grieving process continued, I tried to find ways to make peace with the situation. Taking a sabbatical from writing was the most logical course of action, at least until my muse decided to return. I did find comfort in fellow Llewellyn author Kristoffer Hughes's book *The Journey into Spirit: A Pagan's Perspective on Death, Dying & Bereavement*. His expertise as both a coroner and head of the Anglesey Druid Order in Wales, as well as his personal stories of loss and its aftermath, really helped give me a new perspective, and for that I am truly grateful. However, as my coping skills for dealing with the grief I was feeling grew, another problem was beginning to rear its ugly head.

Personal vs. Public

Witnessing the state of the online world over the previous few years had really made me want to limit the amount of work that I put out. I think that for so many people—artists, writers, actors, designers, and so on—our work is very personal to us, and each piece falls somewhere in between "one of our own children" and "a part of our soul laid bare," so we can be quite protective of it. Letting our little birds fly free from their nest only to see them shot out of the sky before they even have a chance at life is a difficult possibility to accept but one that we all have to learn to handle.

What has become overwhelming for me is the growing trend of vicious personal attacks foisted upon people for no apparent reason. When did this become acceptable? There is a vast difference between constructive criticism and defamation of character. I've been fortunate in that very little vitriol has been aimed my way (so far), but seeing the abundance of unwarranted hate spewed at fellow authors or actors or any other creative individual has really given me pause about the nature and scope of my own work. It all paints a rather grim picture of the current condition of humanity.

Since I was at such a vulnerable place in my personal life, it was taking a great deal of energy to even attempt to reemerge into the social arena. Even the simple act of going online and seeing so many people posting attacks against one another was enough to dissuade me from interacting. Logging on to social media for ten minutes would upset me for the rest of the day, so I took a month off and considered a permanent retreat but eventually changed my mind. After much soul-searching and contemplation, I have come to realize several things that have allowed me to rebuild my sense of self and purpose in order to continue my work and move forward as a more empowered individual and Witch. It's my hope that by sharing my voyage out of the doldrums, others might find a faster journey to safer shores.

What has become overwhelming for me is the growing trend of vicious personal attacks foisted upon people for no apparent reason....There is a vast difference between constructive criticism and defamation of character.

Regaining Strength

One of the first things I had to confront was my anger. Beneath all of my sadness over everything going on in my life lay a boiling crucible of frustration and anger that was threatening to consume me. It felt like everything was happening all at once, as though there was a convergence of calamities and harsh outside forces all well beyond my ability to manage, hell-bent on crushing my spirit. I was angry at what happened, at what "should have" been, at what could never be, and at the world for continuing on as though things were fine. I was also angry at the gods for "allowing" such horrible things to occur (both in my life and globally) and at my personal ancestors for not giving me early warning of what was going to happen.

Forcing myself to confront unhealthy emotions was a difficult process. I'd done shadow work before, but all of this made me feel like I was back at square one. Despite my reluctance to engage in magic or ritual, I decided that it was needed for this work. I wrote down all the things that I felt were making me angry, first as a long, rambling journal entry and then individually, on small pieces of paper. Then I contemplated each and every one of them to determine if I'd identified the real issue. This wasn't a one-day process. It took time to properly identify the core issues, and after I'd identified them, each one needed to be dealt with separately. For me, I just held each paper, read the problem aloud, and acknowledged and accepted responsibility for my feelings on the matter.

I think one key here is to remove any amount of shame about how you feel. As humans, we all have times when we feel angry, sad, hateful, sarcastic, vengeful, frightened, etc., and that's fine. We needn't feel shame for feeling angry or petty in the privacy of our own mind. Another key, however, is that just because we feel a certain way does not mean we should act on it. I gave myself permission for my feelings, but then I worked to let them out and let them go. For most of the circumstances surrounding my troubles, there was nothing I could do to alter the situation, and that was another aspect of my pain. After this, too, had been acknowledged, I had to accept my feeling of powerlessness in that instance and instead take back my power in the form of letting go of my shame and hurt about that fact. For this, I worked the simple rite of burning each paper in my cauldron as a final release of its energy. This doesn't have to be done all at once or on any kind of strict time frame.

Each of us has to be in charge of our own progress. Our individual magical journey is ours alone and needn't be compared to any other. A quote that helped me (which is commonly attributed to Confucius) says, "It does not matter how slow you go as long as you do not stop." As I continued, I came to realize that spirit and divinity hadn't abandoned me, but rather that I'd moved away from them. With time, divination (tarot, pendulum, and scrying), ritual, and proper apologies given, I once again felt their presence in my life and my magic. I came to understand that magic, though powerful, isn't meant to subvert destiny.

I have found working with my pendulum to be particularly helpful because it can provide a means of direct communication with spirit, albeit in a yes-no fashion. A simple ritual to maximize the pendulum's effectiveness is to light a black or white candle in a cauldron to protect against any incorrect or harmful energies. Burning a high-vibration incense such as frankincense helps to invite the proper spirits in, and if you are trying to contact a specific spirit, items associated with the spirit should be placed nearby. From there, reach out with your heart, focusing on the feeling of speaking to them face to face. When ready, ask your questions and write down the answers. This method can facilitate a surprising amount of healing and acceptance.

After I made peace with my inner turmoil, it was time to confront my reluctance to write again and to connect to the online world. Frankly, my motivation was almost nonexistent. The internet has become a vital component of networking, connecting, and exchanging information, particularly for smaller marginalized groups like Pagans, so I decided to make a return to social media. My strategy was to be extremely discerning in my interactions. Though I feel it is important to stay informed and aware of the larger world, I made the choice to strictly limit my social media connections to people and groups that are uplifting and share similar interests. I decided to avoid those obligatory associations with people whose worldviews are staunchly opposed to my lifestyle and religious and political beliefs. This step alone was a huge incentive for me to continue to share my work with others. This whole journey has taught me something about the nature of motivation.

Motivation Found

I think that a lot of us are conditioned to believe that motivation is like divine inspiration and will somehow strike on its own and suddenly bestow upon us enough desire and willpower to reach our goals with ease, but it's almost never that simple. True motivation is an incremental thing, a continuous process fueled by correct actions. In other words, each step taken toward a goal builds a stronger desire to continue on that path. Conversely, steps taken against a goal will only serve to further dissuade a person from trying to reach their objective. Rather than continuing to look forever outward for willpower, validation, or motivation, I learned that these things are not external and cannot be found in the next diet, the next blog post, or the next new trend or purchase. Instead, they can only be found within and, once cultivated, can bring us a resurgence of power and purpose.

Michael Furie (*Northern California*) *is the author of* Supermarket Sabbats, Spellcasting for Beginners, Supermarket Magic, Spellcasting: Beyond the Basics, *and more, all from Llewellyn. A practicing Witch for more than twenty years, he is a priest of the Cailleach. He can be found online at www.michaelfurie.com.*

Witchy Living

Day-by-Day Witchcraft

Workplace Magick

Melanie Marquis

We all have work we have to do, whether it's a personal project, caring for the home and family, or working at a job for much of the day, for multiple days each week. Work is most often a matter of necessity rather than a choice, but we can still choose to utilize the opportunity afforded by our job and enjoy the time we spend working as much as possible. Experienced witches know that the use of magick isn't restricted to the circle. Magick can and should be incorporated into our everyday lives to help ourselves and the world around us to thrive, succeed, and grow. Practicing workplace magick can help you succeed at your job, breeze past obstacles, and enjoy more opportunities to positively affect the world around you with your witchcraft. Here are some ways to use magick to make your job easier and to help you make the most of it, whatever your job may be.

Magickal Tools of the Trade

One subtle yet highly effective and versatile way to work magick while you work is to enchant the tools of your trade. Whether your tools are hammers and circular saws or pencils and laptops, casting charms into the equipment you use in your job can produce both immediate and long-term effects and benefits. Are you a line cook hoping for a smooth night of perfect food? Charm your spatulas, spoons, and other utensils with speed and precision. Are you a veterinarian or nurse with a desire to ease the anxiety of your patients? Charge your stethoscope or other equipment with a calming, soothing vibe. Are you a shop owner wishing to increase sales? Cast a spell on your cash register to attract money, or charm your inventory to make it irresistible. If you have business cards, try enchanting them to return to you in the form of clients and profits.

To enchant the tools of your trade, think of your intention as you touch the object or place your hand near it. Imagine the effect you desire taking place as clearly and vividly as you can, putting both emotion and vision into your intention. Allow these thoughts and feelings to flow into the object to program it with your will. It might help you to visualize this energy as a stream of colored light, pulsating in synchronicity with your wish. The more emotion and energy you can put into your vision, the stronger the magick will be. Though it's nice to spend more time doing this if you're able, this is a charm that can be cast in an instant without anyone around you knowing what you're up to.

Thoughtful Threads

Choosing your work clothes with magick in mind can also provide benefits. Whether you employ color symbolism, patterns, or other methods, your wardrobe affects not only your mood but also your luck and the way you're perceived by others. Want to attract money? Wear green, gold, or silver clothing or accessories to align with a prosperous flow. Want to create a calm feeling in yourself and appear trustworthy to others? Choose brown or other earth tones. Wearing dark blue will help you convey an air of authority, while wearing a pastel shade of sky blue or sea green will encourage cooperation from those around you. If protection from gossiping or ill-intentioned coworkers is what you're after, choose black or boldly patterned clothing to help deflect and diffuse the negativity.

Witches who have to wear a uniform or adhere to a dress code at work can still find discreet ways to maximize the magickal potential of their clothing. You might choose your underclothes with color symbolism in mind, or tuck a sprig of rosemary into the cuffs of your shirt to help you maintain a joyful, positive attitude. For some extra luck during your work shift or for success at an important meeting or job interview, you might put a piece of John the Conqueror root in your pocket, or place a gold star sticker on the inside or soles of your shoes. If jewelry is an option, you might wear a jade ring or pendant to enhance your leadership qualities, a tiger's eye stone to increase your confidence, or a clear quartz crystal to boost your energy and personal power. With a little creativity, a limited wardrobe doesn't have to limit your magickal options.

Enchanting the Workspace

Whatever your work environment, it's possible to transform it with a little magick. Changing the vibe of your workplace can positively affect the working dynamic, attract customers, create a more supportive

and cooperative atmosphere, increase profits, and more. Just as a person might charge a crystal or other stone, filling it with intention and energy, so too can the working witch enchant their workspace. Are you a server in a restaurant, hoping to earn big tips? Try casting a charm into the tables and chairs to inspire generosity in your diners. Do you want everyone who comes to your store to enjoy a boost of good luck? Hang a lucky charm in the doorway, or imbue the welcome mat with a joyful energy of attraction and abundance. Do you work outdoors at a construction site? Consider casting a protective field of energy around the space to help keep everyone safe and avoid accidents.

Do you work in an office with a bunch of grumpy coworkers? You might discreetly charm everyone's laptop or desk with a peaceful, calming vibe.

To enchant your workspace, just think of the intended result you want to achieve and picture this happening as clearly as you can, feeling the emotions and experiencing the energy that would come with it.

To enchant your workspace, just think of the intended result you want to achieve and picture this happening as clearly as you can, feeling the emotions and experiencing the energy that would come with it. You can either send this energy to surround the space as a whole or cast it into objects in the workspace, such as counters, photocopy machines, and even the walls and flooring. As a human, you have the natural ability to move and transform energy, so trust in that and know that your intentions will go where you tell them to go, informing your workspace to get in alignment with your goals.

Dealing with Issues

No matter how hard we try at our jobs, there are bound to be problems that arise from time to time. Whether it's an issue that seems to have no solution or a problem coworker who sows hostility in the workplace, using magick can help you overcome troubles and find your way around obstacles. Are you facing a problem at your work for which you haven't been able to come up with a solution? Try using divination or dream magick to gain new insights and a fresh perspective. You might focus on the problem and mix your tarot deck as you think, *What is the solution?* Draw a few cards and meditate for a few minutes to see if any new ideas pop into your head or if there are any obvious solutions suggested by the cards. Alternatively, you might write a description of the problem on a slip of paper and place this under your pillow at night before you sleep, knowing that a solution might present itself in your dreams. When you wake up, write down everything you can remember from your dreams. Once you're fully awake, look back at what you wrote and see if there are any insights into your problem.

Is your workplace fraught with negativity that impacts your ability to do your job? Try placing a piece of jet and a citrine crystal on your desk, or carry the stones in your pocket. The jet will absorb the negative vibes, while the citrine will impart a cheerful, positive, purifying energy. Do you ever feel the need to calm and center yourself at work due to stressful situations that crop up? Keep a rose quartz in your pocket that you can touch to absorb a peaceful, loving vibration.

Putting Your Work to Work

However you look at it, work is an exchange of energy. We do what's expected of us, and in return we receive financial compensation and other rewards. Allowing magick to be a part of your work life can make this exchange of energy much more balanced and beneficial for you and for the world at large. We are channels of a universal energy of wisdom and love, and we can make each interaction with others, each act of service, or each product we produce a reflection of this wisdom and love. This is what is meant by "walking the talk" or "living your Craft." Magick is an integral part of who we are, and one that we cannot separate ourselves from. We witches are weavers of the fabric of reality, and we all have important work to do.

Melanie Marquis *is the creator of the* Modern Spellcaster's Tarot *(illustrated by Scott Murphy) and the author of several books, including* A Witch's World of Magick; The Witch's Bag of Tricks; Carl Llewellyn Weschcke: Pioneer and Publisher of Body, Mind & Spirit; Witchy Mama *(with Emily A. Francis);* Beltane; *and* Lughnasadh. *The founder of United Witches Global Coven and a local coordinator for the Pagan Pride Project, Melanie loves sharing magick with others and has presented workshops and rituals to audiences across the US. She lives in Denver, Colorado.*

Survival Guide for the
Solitary Suburban Witch

Ember Grant

Does this sound familiar? You're in your backyard—on your deck, perhaps, or your patio—and you've planned to work some magic or conduct a peaceful, solitary ritual. Suddenly the roar of a lawn mower rips through the silence or the kids across the street start screaming, and your magical focus is broken. You go inside, but the mood is gone. You can't feel the sunlight or see the moonlight; you can't feel the breeze or hear the birds. So much for practicing magic in a natural space.

Witches in the suburbs face a special set of challenges. We're in between city and country life. Chances are there's little privacy for outdoor magic and rituals, and not much peace and quiet when you want it. There are, of course, varying levels of privacy in the suburbs. Some neighborhoods can be quite peaceful and have spacious yards, but in others the homes are so close together that you can literally look out your window and into your neighbor's house. Some have trees, some don't; some neighborhoods even prohibit privacy fences.

Even if we like our neighbors, they're still going to make noise at times when it's inconvenient for us. Really, there are only two things to do, aside from moving: ignore them and proceed with your business (which may be difficult or impossible) or find ways to work around them. That's the main strategy I propose—learning how to work around the distractions. Let's face it, we can't choose our neighbors, and it's in our best interest to get along with them. There are many options for coping. Some of them depend on your specific situation, but many apply to everyone. Ultimately, we are responsible for accepting our situation and making the best of it.

Most witches are adept at creating magical environments, both inside and out, but these are the situations that really test our creativity. As a pagan, I want to be close to nature whenever possible for my rituals. I also want the convenience of being at home. I grew up in a rural setting, with the peace and quiet of nature all around me, but since then I've lived in several different suburban neighborhoods. But regardless of the living situation—whether in a house, apartment, or cottage—there are always the same main challenges: privacy and noise. So I've developed some strategies for dealing with these difficult situations.

Finding Peace and Quiet

First, let's discuss noise, which may be the biggest challenge. Unless you have your own plot of land, you're going to hear other people or traffic or some form of distraction. One helpful strategy is to get to know

Take advantage of inclement weather. Seriously. Since most people escape indoors when it's raining, make it your mission to get outside during that time.

the patterns around you. What are the quiet times in your neighborhood? Are there days when you're home and everyone else is at work? Are mornings quiet, or maybe late evenings, after the kids are in bed? Observe the routines of your neighbors to know the times when they tend to be outside. This doesn't mean stalking them! Just notice things. Summers are difficult in my neighborhood because my next-door neighbor is a teacher and she's home in the summer with her young children, so they're outside quite a bit. But when she goes back to school and the kids are in daycare, the days get quiet.

Take advantage of inclement weather. Seriously. Since most people escape indoors when it's raining, make it your mission to get outside during that time. The best-case scenario is that you have a covered area of some kind—under a deck, a gazebo (you can even put curtains on it!), or even a simple patio umbrella will do. If you don't have these options, consider investing in one. Canvas gazebos are popular, and there are some reasonably priced ones on the market. Also, on really hot or cold days, when it's uncomfortable, try to make peace with the discomfort. I hate the heat, but when it's 100 degrees, I know my neighbors won't be outside.

Finally, don't forget about earplugs and headphones. Put on your favorite music to mask the noise, or use earplugs to block out as much as possible. I've done this many times when I wanted to be outside but I could hear the neighborhood noise. My patio has quite a bit of visual privacy, but there's no escaping the sound of other people. I have a waterfall fountain and it helps, but it's not enough, so sometimes I have to resort to this option if I really want to enjoy my outdoor space.

Preserving Privacy

Beyond the noise issues, there's privacy. Some people live in a place where their backyard is visible to everyone around them. If you don't have trees or a fence, how can you make a private outdoor space for ritual? It goes without saying that investing in trees and shrubs is a good idea. Yes, it takes time for them to grow, but it's worth it if you plan on staying in your home for a long time. In the meantime, or for a quick fix, large potted plants, trellises, and other outdoor features can do the trick. Strategically placed plants can work wonders.

If you're concerned about your props and tools being seen, there are easy ways around that. Plant stands can serve as altars, and garden statuary, rock gardens with crystals, and other popular deck and patio features give you a wide range of options. Your magical tools can hide in plain sight. I have an outdoor altar that is basically a small concrete table. (It's actually an old birdbath turned upside down.) I keep a potted plant and a crystal cluster on it. It looks like a decorative plant stand to anyone who might see it. When I need to use it, it's easy to add a candle or some incense and work outdoors.

Subtle decorative lighting is another way to take advantage of the outdoors. Maybe night is the best time for you to work magic outside, but you need to see and don't want a bright spotlight or porch light announcing your presence. Use decorative garden lighting, such as string lights or battery candles, or arrange a few lanterns in your outdoor space. Lanterns are also an excellent way to keep real candles burning in windy situations. Fire pits are perfect too. They're all the rage in suburban backyards and you can use them in your rituals.

Finally, it's okay to admit defeat—sometimes you just have to retreat indoors. Maybe your neighbors decided to have a party at the exact same time you planned a quiet outdoor ritual in the backyard. There's really nothing you can do about that. They have a right to entertain their friends. If what you're doing depends on precise timing, you'll just have to go inside or elsewhere. If it doesn't, wait to have your ritual another night.

Another way to cope is to bring the outside in. I do this quite often. Play a recording of bird sounds, crickets, or a rainstorm. Get a small water fountain, or turn off the lights and light candles. Use plants—both indoor ones and plants outside that you can view through a window—to complete the illusion. If you have a windowsill, fill it with plants and crystals. Create a simulated outdoor space in your home. I decorated the deck outside my dining room so that plants and flowers are visible when I'm inside. If it's too noisy to be outdoors, I can sit inside and look out the window at my little oasis on the deck. I see the flowers, magical statues, crystals tucked into potted plants, and a small fountain, and I can watch hummingbirds visit the feeder—even if I can't be outside.

If the situation becomes truly disruptive, as a last resort you may have to complain to a higher authority. Let's hope it doesn't come to that. First, talk to your neighbors if you're comfortable doing so. Of course, I realize this isn't always feasible. Know your city's ordinances as well. If there's an actual violation, call the authorities. You can do this anonymously, but be sure it's really necessary. If the situation is really bad and beyond your control, file a formal complaint. Hopefully, though, the situations you face can be dealt with by developing creative coping strategies to get you through. When my neighbors are being

> I decorated the deck outside my dining room so that plants and flowers are visible when I'm inside. If it's too noisy to be outdoors, I can sit inside and look out the window at my little oasis on the deck.

noisy, I remind myself that they can't be outside all the time. When they go back in, I'll go out, even if it means doing so late at night, early in the morning, or when the temperature is less than desirable.

And now the big question: Should you use magic on your neighbors? It depends. I've done this on two occasions. Both were the result of dealing with repeated offenses over time (some of which involved the authorities). Both of those neighbors ended up moving. Save your binding and banishing for extreme situations, but you should always defend yourself and your right to privacy, peace, and quiet. Just ask yourself first if there are mundane ways to deal with it. The occasional party is going to happen. Dogs bark and kids play. But if the dog is barking for three hours nonstop, perhaps someone needs to look into the situation. Get creative and find ways to cope.

You have a right to enjoy your outside space, just as they do. With compromise and patience, hopefully everyone can find peace—and you can have a magical suburban backyard.

Ember Grant *has been writing for the Llewellyn annuals since 2003 and is the author of three books:* Magical Candle Crafting, The Book of Crystal Spells, *and* The Second Book of Crystal Spells. *She lives in Missouri with her husband and two feline companions. Visit her at EmberGrant.com.*

Magickal Calisthenics: Simple Workings to Improve Your Magick Skills

Emily Carlin

When people ask me how they can improve their magickal skills, my answer is always the same: practice, practice some more, and then practice a bit more. No matter what you'd like to do better—divination, energy work, spirit communication, etc.—the only way to develop your magickal muscles is to actually do those things. This doesn't mean performing large, complex magickal rites every Tuesday. It means doing small, simple magickal workings on a regular basis as a form of magickal calisthenics.

While magick can be done quickly and easily, it should always be performed mindfully, with the end result carefully considered. When an individual learns to bake a cake, they must put together ingredients, bake them, and then deal with the cake once it's baked. If they need to bake thirty cakes to

While magick can be done quickly and easily, it should always be performed mindfully, with the end result carefully considered.

learn how to do it, they've got to figure out what to do with thirty cakes. Learning to cast a spell or make a charm is no different: you gather materials and energies (ingredients), infuse them with your will (baking), and then release them into the world to create the desired effect (the finished cake).

Just as most people don't really want thirty cakes in their home, most people don't really want thirty scrying mirrors or job-finding charms either. Similarly, when learning a new skill, most people begin with inexpensive materials (construction paper, plastic beads, etc.) and work their way up to more expensive ones (handmade paper, crystal beads, etc.) as their proficiency increases. In magick, this translates as both physical materials (herbs, crystals, tools, etc.) and energetic cost. Large or complex workings require a lot of time and energy, regardless of the physical materials used, making them less suitable for day-to-day practice than simpler exercises that are less energetically expensive. In deciding what types of magick to do as a routine practice, it is best to choose small exercises that are more effective when done over time rather than larger workings designed for big one-time payoffs or exercises that result in a unique physical object each time.

The best magickal practices to be used as calisthenics should also have universally desirable results. Magick causes change in the world, so you must be certain you actually want that change to occur. Unlike other skills, magick is virtually impossible to practice without actually doing it. As with the contents of Pandora's box, once energy is released into the world, it's pretty much impossible to call back again. Intent and will very rarely accept "oops" or "I didn't mean it" and undo themselves. That means you must be extremely careful with how you practice as you learn. The exercises outlined here are designed to be positive workings that will be beneficial to virtually anyone at virtually any time. Universal things like good health, prosperity, and good fortune can benefit all practitioners. As the results of these exercises are almost always desirable, it's pretty much always appropriate to do them.

Weekly Magickal Exercises

Here are a few quick magickal exercises to strengthen your core magickal abilities—one for each day of the week.

Note: All of these exercises can and should be tweaked to fit with your current practices or magickal system. These can be done daily, once a week, or in whatever frequency and combination works best for you. For maximum effect, no more than one exercise per day is recommended.

Monday—Divination

Do a simple divination of "What do I need to know about the coming week?" or "Where should I focus my energies this week?" using whatever form of divination you wish to increase your skill in.

This can be a single-card tarot draw, a single rune or bone draw, a tea leaf reading, etc. Confine this exercise to simple single interpretation readings rather than multi-object spreads or in-depth explorations of a topic. This exercise is less about the information you receive during

the reading and more about becoming comfortable with the method of divination and recognizing the energies of divination. It can be helpful to write down the results of the divination and how you felt while doing it in order to recognize patterns in the information and to better understand how your energies move while divining.

TUESDAY—PROTECTION

Cast a basic bubble shield and hold it for a set duration of time.

Learning to shield is a vital way of maintaining your energetic health and integrity in a world awash with negative and foreign energies. If you are already comfortable with a particular type of shield, feel free to use that. Otherwise, use the basic bubble shield as follows. Imagine a solid bubble of energy forming all the way around your body, creating a barrier through which negative energy cannot penetrate. As you picture a solid egg of energy forming around you, feel the air around you thicken with energy or imagine a particular smell filling the space around you. This simple shield will protect you as long as you hold it in your mind. When you stop holding the shield in your mind, it will fade away. Begin by consciously holding the shield for five minutes, then allow it to dissipate and the energy to ground. Over time, you can lengthen the amount of time that you hold the shield.

WEDNESDAY—COMMUNICATION

Perform a verbal or nonverbal spell to strengthen your communication skills.

We all have to communicate with others and we all benefit from being as clear and effective in our communications as possible. Choose an area of communication in which you'd like to improve: in-person, phone, online, spirit communication, psychic communication, etc. Create a short verbal incantation, a series of movements, or a sigil empowered to aid you in your goal. For example, to strengthen in-person communication, recite the following incantation: *My voice communicates what I intend, and it is understood as I intend by those who hear it.* To strengthen written communication, write the incantation on a piece of paper and burn it. To strengthen nonverbal or energetic communication, create a series of gestures or dance steps infused with your intent and perform them. For maximum effect, either focus on your weakest skill or regularly switch off between strengthening verbal and nonverbal communication to maintain balance.

THURSDAY—LUCK

Create or charge a good luck charm.

Everyone can use a little extra luck in their lives—that little something to smooth the way and just make things easier. If you don't already have a charm or talisman that you carry for luck, choose an object that you can easily carry on your person that represents luck or prosperity to you. Something that can be worn as jewelry, carried in a pocket, or worn on the inside of your clothing is ideal. For example, you could choose a citrine pendant, a game token, a twenty-sided die, a special key, or a milagro. Coins can work well, but you must take care not to spend them accidentally (or you will have to recreate the charm). If you choose a coin or something coin-shaped, go for oversized coins, foreign coins, poker chips, and the like. Enchant your chosen object with luck and prosperity energy and carry it with you throughout the week. This is a great opportunity to practice using an anointing oil, such as bay or bergamot essential oil, if you choose. Once made, the object can be re-energized each week.

FRIDAY—LOVE AND RELATIONSHIPS

Perform a cord magick spell for improved relationships.

Our lives consist of many relationships, be they with family, friends, coworkers, or significant others, and we all want those relationships to be as healthy and nourishing as possible. For this exercise, you can create one cord to represent all of your relationships, make a cord a week for each type of relationship you want to strengthen, or make specific cords for specific relationships, depending on what best serves your needs. Get a length of cord or string, six to twelve inches long, in a neutral color (white or natural is best, though you can coordinate the color of the cord with what corresponds best to your intention for the relationship). Tie a series of seven knots in the cord, one for each quality you'd like to bring to your relationship, such as the following: (1) respect, (2) empathy/understanding, (3) caring, (4) affection, (5) support, (6) happiness, and (7) longevity. The last knot should tie the end of the cord to the beginning of it to create a circle. You can create a new cord each week or simply recharge the knots on an existing cord by focusing your intent and touching each knot while repeating the quality it represents.

Saturday—Cleansing

Perform a cleansing bath.

Every day we wade through the energies of the world, and for good or ill, we end up taking some of that energy home with us. In order to maintain our equilibrium, it is important to regularly cleanse our energies of that which is not our own in order to better know and strengthen ourselves. One of the easiest and most effective ways to do this is to incorporate psychic cleansing into your regular shower or bath. To do so, perform your ablutions as usual while mentally holding the intent of energetic dirt being washed away with the physical dirt. At the end of your shower or bath, scoop a handful of water over your head and visualize it taking any remaining energetic detritus with it as it runs down your body

In order to maintain our equilibrium, it is important to regularly cleanse our energies of that which is not our own in order to better know and strengthen ourselves.

and into the drain. Feel free to boost the effectiveness of your cleansing by using salt scrubs, essential oils, or special soaps.

Sunday—Health

Perform a kitchen magick spell for improved or maintained health.

We all know that eating nourishing food is good for our health, so infusing healthful and healing energies into that food can only be helpful. Prepare a healthy piece of food or a drink. (A simple piece of fruit or a cup of tea is fine if you're not culinarily inclined.) As you prepare the food or drink, focus your intent on the image of "perfect health," whatever that looks like for you. Allow that healthful energy to flow into the food or drink and enhance its natural nourishing properties. This process can be as simple as smiling while stirring honey into your tea or as elaborate as infusing energy into every step of making puff pastry. Do whatever best fits your needs and kitchen habits. Once the energy is infused into the finished food or drink, consume it as usual.

· · · · · · · · · · · ·

The best magickal practices to be used as calisthenics are energetically low-cost, are effective in small doses over time, and have desirable cumulative results. The exercises presented here are merely suggestions from the myriad practices available to choose from. Start with these simple practices and then adapt and change them as your skills develop. Explore the many magickal exercises in the world and create your own magickal calisthenics routine to suit your personal practice and desire for growth.

Emily Carlin *is a Witch, writer, teacher, mediator, and ritual presenter based in Seattle, Washington. She currently teaches one-on-one online and at in-person events on the West Coast. For more information and links to her blogs, go to https://about.me/ecarlin.*

Walking and Running as a Magickal Act

Jason Mankey

Though Witchcraft often romanticizes rural areas and the agrarian way of life, most of today's practitioners live in cities and suburbs. Strip malls, high-rises, condominiums, freeways, traffic lights…Modern conveniences are great, but they don't do much to connect us to the natural world or the Wheel of the Year. Luckily, there's an easy fix for this problem that most of us are probably going to do every day anyway: walking and/or running.

I've never been a big fan of bicycles or cars, so for most of my life I've used my feet to get wherever I need to go. If something is within three miles of my house (or a train station), I generally walk there. There's just so much more to see and experience while on your feet and not behind the wheel of a car. Even in the urban jungle, the natural world is alive and showing us her magick and mystery, if we just take time to look.

I am not a particularly good runner but took up the practice again recently. Several knee injuries suffered in high school rendered me incapable of running for almost twenty years, but thanks to my wife's excellent health care plan and an imaginative doctor, I recently found my running shoes again and jog (poorly) most mornings around my Northern California home. My morning runs have become a treasured activity and are one of the most witchy things I do most days.

When outdoors on my two feet, I experience the world through most of my five senses (taste doesn't really come into play most days since I don't lick trees) and my sensitivities as a Witch. Any space with at least a couple of trees and a patch or two of weeds can become a transformative cauldron for the Witch who takes the time to be aware of their surroundings and truly appreciate them. Opening yourself up to what's truly around you is a balm for the soul and a way to strengthen your relationship with the natural world and the Craft.

See

The most obvious sense to use while walking is sight. We have to pay attention to where we are going so we don't get hit by a car or stumble on an uneven piece of sidewalk, but there's so much going on outside beyond those concerns. Trees are probably the most attention-grabbing of nature's attractions, and seeing the same tree daily over the course of a year or two will reveal a lot about your local environment. It's awe-inspiring to know just when a tree buds, when its leaves become fully

formed, and finally, when its leaves are about to fall to the ground. This is something we so often take for granted, but it's so marvelous! It's the entire Wheel of the Year (birth, life, death, and rebirth) played out right in front of us!

But there's so much more out there than trees. Various flowers and weeds bloom throughout the year, all with their own magickal properties. After spotting a new plant, it's fun to try to figure out just what it might be and how it could be useful in ritual and magick. There's also the waxing and waning of the sun throughout the year. No matter how warm or cold a region might be, the amount of sunlight it gets is a direct connection to the turning of the seasons. I don't get snow where I live in California, but I know it's winter here when dawn cloaks my neighborhood until 9:00 a.m.

Hear

Those of us who live in cities and suburbs probably hear the rattle and hum of cars more than anything else, but there are other sounds out there that can connect us directly to nature. There are not a lot of bugs where I live in California, but there are crickets, and I can just about tell you what month it is based on their chirping. The crickets all but disappear in the winter, then slowly reemerge in March, and finally reach a crescendo in September and October. They have their preferred haunts too, and their sounds often disappear and reappear over the course of six or seven city blocks.

Sound travels differently depending on the time of year. In the summer heat, when the air is full of water, its reach is far less. The trains that cross the railroad tracks five blocks from my house are hard to hear in the summer, but in the winter they come in as clear as their whistles. Over the course of the year, it's fun to hear how they rise and fall in intensity.

Perhaps the most startling thing to learn when we truly listen to the world is just how quiet it can be in winter. Even though sound travels more easily in the cold air, the lack of activity by bugs, birds, and even humans often results in a near-sacred hush around Yuletide. And then slowly over the next few weeks and months the volume of nature rises again, and by Beltane it sounds like everything around me is once again in a festive mood.

Smell

While few of us think of scent as one of our most powerful senses, it's the one I perhaps notice the most, and take the most satisfaction in, while running. There's the perfume of fresh jasmine in late May, its scent often more potent than that of any scented candle. Dead, dry grass is the smell of early autumn in California, a scent that often makes me melancholy. Sadly, the scent of dry grass these days is often intermixed with that of smoke from California's numerous wildfires (the result of global warming), which reminds me to be aware of and involved in fighting climate change.

"Unpleasant" odors also have their own rewards. The scent of decaying leaves in early spring is a promise of the life to come as the world grows warmer and the days longer. Reclaimed swampland often has its own musk after a heavy rain, and the rotting scent of the San Francisco Bay serves to remind me of just how close I am to the Pacific Ocean. Scent can help connect us to the wider world around us, far beyond what we can see or hear.

Touch

Touch can be subtle. We often don't notice it unless it's especially pleasurable or painful, but it's always there. Every time we are outside, there's the heat or the cold of the air pressing against our bodies and filling our lungs. Cold air is especially hard to breathe in while running, and is another reminder of the challenges many of us face in the winter. The sweat I develop on a warm morning run makes me feel primal and alive, much like the world around me at that time of year.

Heat and cold are among the most obvious things we feel when we are outdoors, but there's more out there that can be experienced. Your itchy and watery eyes will let you know when allergy season is near (or has peaked), and a wet breeze might feel like a greeting from a river, ocean, or lake. The feeling of the ground beneath our feet will vary from season to season too, depending on how wet the ground is and how much grass is growing on it. Sometimes it's like a soft carpet and other times like a hard tile floor. Rain can feel

> **Rain can feel soothing or violent depending on its intensity, and this knowledge can be used in magickal workings. (Stormy weather, stormy magick!)**

soothing or violent depending on its intensity, and this knowledge can be used in magickal workings. (Stormy weather, stormy magick!)

Our Witch Senses

At Samhain, the phrase "the veil is thin" (referring to the boundary between the living and the dead) is nearly a mantra, but it's not an exaggeration. The thinning veil is something we can *feel* when we are outside, and its shifts are noticeable on a day-to-day basis. If we open up all of our senses, it's possible to feel the souls of those we have lost lingering on the breeze or perhaps even running or walking beside us. In the fall and winter months, the veil ebbs and flows just a little bit, with its boundary sometimes stronger or weaker for whatever reason. The smart Witch knows when to take advantage of these moments in order to leave a gift for their ancestors or ask a boon of a deceased loved one.

The spirits of the dead aren't the only things we can sense when we bring our Witch senses into play. All around us are spirits of place and the fey, powers that have had to adjust and adapt due to humanity's desire to constantly reconstruct the natural world. Simply acknowledging the fair folk can bring about their aid and blessings. Most humans aren't instinctive or smart enough to seek out what lies beyond their cell phone screen, but Witches know better. There's an entire magickal world awaiting us every time we leave our home, if we are just willing to look.

Jason Mankey is a Wiccan-Witch who lives in Northern California with his wife, Ari, and two cats. He is the author of Transformative Witchcraft: The Greater Mysteries, along with several books in The Witch's Tools series. He writes online at the blog Raise the Horns (https://www.patheos.com/blogs/panmankey/).

Bringing Back Hospitality: How to Create a Welcoming Community

Blake Octavian Blair

We all desire to be part of a welcoming community and to feel taken care of and valued. But do you? Do you attend an event or visit a group and find yourself feeling left in the cold? Do you do what you can to be welcoming to others?

In this modern age, we are often faced with conversations on how we can engage in better community building and what qualities we desire in our communities. A key ingredient to create a welcoming community is hospitality. We say we want a community that is hospitable, yet we often find a lack in that area. So what is the solution? How do we bring back a sense of hospitality that people talk about from the days of yore?

Hospitality as a Value

Many spiritual cultures include hospitality as a core value. Alexei Kondratiev, a linguist and teacher of Celtic cultures and languages, said that hospitality was one of the six core values of the Celts, the others being honesty, courage, justice, loyalty, and honor (Isaac 2016). That is a list with some pretty weighty moral company! Some hypothesize that the Celtic emphasis on hospitality might harken back to the time when the Celts were nomadic and they experienced hospitality in the homes of kind folks along their travels.

Many tell of the traditional practice of offering a guest the best seat in the home. In cold seasons, this is often the seat closest to the hearth fire, the reason for this being that the prized seat of honor is multilayered. On a basic level, it is warm and dry. On a deeper level, it is putting your guest nearest to the sacred hearth and to deities held dear, such as Brigid.

These types of traditions seem hardwired into some Celtic lines. For example, my mum-in-law tells stories of my grandma (her mom), who hailed from Scotland, always keeping the finest she had of everything ready to offer to guests. Whether it was a drink, towels, or bed linens, it was the best of what she had on hand. When a guest would appear at her home, Grandma seemed to produce tea and assorted cookies and biscuits, at the very least, at a moment's notice. Her reasoning: "It's just what you do!"

Buddhism also places an emphasis on being hospitable. Atithisatkara, a Sanskrit term that appears throughout Buddhist texts, loosely translates to "doing something good for a guest." Buddhist texts also mention

on occasion the importance of unplanned giving, for it is easy for many to give if they plan in advance but it is truly a test when they are in a position where it must be extended unexpectedly. This is where we demonstrate whether we walk our talk and live our spirituality as a way of life or it's just a hat that we occasionally put on.

Lost and Found: Hospitality

However, based on the experiences of my mum-in-law and of many of my friends and peers, it seems that hospitality has somehow been lost in time or in translation, or both, in our modern-day communities. Hypotheses abound as to why it has largely gone by the wayside, from people's attachment to smartphones and technology to the transient nature of our culture. But I posit that none of these are actually acceptable reasons for the forgoing of hospitality.

Many spiritual groups and communities are incredibly close, but they can become exclusionary and insular if we are not careful. Groups can become so tight-knit that they lose the ability to know how to welcome visitors or outsiders.

What can be done? Well, when hospitality is instilled in us and exercised on an individual level, as part of our personal ethos, it can naturally spread and expand among groups and communities. For the most immediate results, we can explore accessible solutions on the individual level.

One of the simplest things we can do is to extend our attention to a person. Give them both a voice and an audience. Do not be glued to your smartphone screen for the entire interaction. If you're in a group where there is a newcomer, invite them into the conversation and ask their opinion. It can be incredibly difficult for a newcomer to join in among a group of established comrades. This is perhaps the simplest way we can extend our hospitality to a stranger in almost any setting, whether one-on-one or in a group.

In our own home, we perhaps can take the most control of the situation. For most of us, by the time we allow somebody into our home, we have established some level of association or connection with them, whether they are a close friend, an associate of a coven or grove, or perhaps a member of a club we belong to. If we take advantage of the opportunity, these connections allow us to be even more hospitable. Where to begin extending hospitality to guests in the home? Offering a guest a drink and a comfortable seat is a great place to begin. Making a guest comfortable will put them at ease and make them feel welcome and valued.

Hospitality on Equal Footing

In many modern strains of paganism, there is a growing level of egalitarianism between clergy and laypeople. This is often the case in modern Buddhism as well. Clergy and monastic people are worthy of our respect and acknowledgment; however, in terms of status, there is an increasing leveling of the field and they are no longer exalted as "superhuman." So hospitality is a two-way street, and in searching for ways to be hospitable, we can use the Golden Rule as a rule of thumb—yes, the good old cross-cultural adage that you should treat others the way you wish to be treated yourself. All people who treat you with kindness and respect are worthy of your hospitality.

Another cue we can take from the ethos of these long-standing cultures is that of being willing to extend hospitality unexpectedly. Religious texts across traditions are full of tales of the arrival of unexpected guests, sometimes monastics and occasionally in disguise. One who seems to be a common passerby turns out to be a monk or even a god. The phrase *Atithi devo bhava*, taken from ancient Hindu scripture, loosely means "the guest is God." In modern paganism, we often stress the divine spark that lives within each of us, so this is a very relatable bit of theology. Sometimes community members and loved ones need our hospitality without notice for a myriad of reasons. They might need a safe place with a listening ear and a cup of tea for an hour, or a place to stay for the night. We don't always have any lead time, and how we react in these situations, within our means, can be a test of our hospitality.

Challenging Your Hospitality

Hosting overnight guests can be a challenge on many levels. Navigating meals, sleeping accommodations, and even personality conflicts are considerations. (We all have family members we love but have personality conflicts with in close quarters.) Advice on managing personality conflicts could be an entire additional article, so I'll only briefly discuss it here. It is not uncommon to have more in common with our chosen family and friends than with our blood relatives. When you do encounter a guest with vastly different views, things will go best if all involved can respect differences of opinion. A good strategy is to steer the conversation toward more common and benign topics. Opinions are rarely changed over the short term or in heated conversations. We may want to do our best to open the mind of our politically or religiously conservative Great-Aunt Velma, but that battle isn't likely to be won during a two-day visit over Thanksgiving. We must take care not to allow our differences to affect our hospitality. Being hospitable does not require us to agree with or approve of our guest's viewpoints and behaviors. Additionally, we need not live inauthentically or tolerate abuse to keep the peace.

When it comes to providing actual physical accommodations for guests, it can be tricky if you live in a small space. However, it can be done. Many guests do not need an elaborate private suite to enjoy your hospitality. When my husband and I lived in a small one-bedroom apartment in Boston, we did not have a lot of space, to say the least. However, we had a comfortable futon sofa in our living room, which we made into a comfortable bed for numerous guests. We cleared a corner of the room for them to put their bags, and we never had any complaints and in fact had many repeat guests.

Of course, personal touches that make your guests feel welcome are important. We always put one of my husband's handmade quilts on the futon for them, and good, soft linens. Now that we own a house, we actually have a full furnished guest bedroom. We offer an endless stream of coffee and tea in our home, and depending on the duration of our guest's stay, we often cook for them. After all, we need to eat ourselves anyway, and including them is not much more trouble, generally. We have had some guests with interesting dietary restrictions, which, when given advance notice, we do our best to accommodate.

Offering hospitality is a way to show love and respect to a fellow human being. Revisiting the lessons of my Scottish grandma-in-law, remember that you do not have to offer the finest of everything that exists,

Offering hospitality is a way to show love and respect to a fellow human being.... Remember that you do not have to offer the finest of everything that exists, but try to offer the best you have.

but try to offer the best you have (in terms of both accommodations and being a warm host) to make them comfortable. If all you have to offer is a sofa for a place to sleep and a glass of ice water for refreshment, then by all means, make the best sleeping accommodations on the sofa to the best of your ability and give them the coolest, most refreshing glass of water you possibly can. For Grandma, it was just part of her Celtic nature to be hospitable. It was just what you did. The simplest acts and offerings can be as powerful as anything that is considered fancy. It's all about the intent behind the gesture you're extending.

Abuse Is Unacceptable

We do need to discuss, however, what hospitality is *not*. Hospitality is not being taken advantage of or living inauthentically due to the presence of guests. While it is a shame that this even has to be discussed, it indeed must. I think every hospitable person has a tale to tell of a nightmare houseguest, such as the guest who arrives to stay overnight and then (over-)extends their visit and doesn't inform the host of what their actual plans are, or the guest who doesn't reveal dietary restrictions until you're already cooking the meal. Then there is the judgmental guest who offers commentary on how you should keep your home, how you cook, your personal religious beliefs, or your political leanings.

You should not feel any pressure to accept abuse. I spoke earlier of not letting differences diminish your hospitality. However, I did qualify that it does not mean living inauthentically and that there needs to be mutual respect for each other. I have plenty of friends, community members, and loved ones I disagree with on some things. However, we always respect each other's opinions. It is rare, but you may come across guests whom you decide are not welcome for a repeat visit to your home if they turn out to be abusive or disrespectful. On rare occasions, you may even have to ask somebody to leave. Thankfully, I have not yet had that most extreme situation arise, but should it, I wouldn't hesitate. Above all, remain true to yourself. When you give of yourself genuinely, it's hard to go wrong.

Consider all of these points when you are in the role of the guest as well. Set your host up for success! Let them know your dietary requirements as far ahead as possible, be honest about how long you plan to stay, and share with them any items on your itinerary that concern their time hosting you. You don't have to avoid ideological differences in conversation, but if you do broach them, try to create an environment of mutual respect.

. . . .

Whether you are the host or the guest, and whether the visit is for a couple hours or overnight, I hope this discussion was helpful. Remember, hospitality is sacred and a magickal act in and of itself!

Resources

Isaac, Ali. "6 Founding Principles of Ancient Irish Society." *Ali Isaac Storyteller*, March 21, 2016. https://aliisaacstoryteller .com/2016/03/21/6-founding-principles-of-ancient-irish-society/.

Kearney, Richard, and James Taylor, eds. *Hosting the Stranger: Between Religions*. New York: Continuum, 2011.

McColman, Carl. "The Heart of Celtic Spirituality Is Hospitality." *Patheos*, June 8, 2017. http://www.patheos.com/blogs/carlmccolman/2017/06 /heart-celtic-spirituality-hospitality/.

Weatherstone, Lunaea. *Tending Brigid's Flame: Awaken to the Celtic Goddess of Hearth, Temple, and Forge*. Woodbury, MN: Llewellyn, 2015.

Blake Octavian Blair *is a shamanic practitioner, ordained minister, writer, Usui Reiki Master-Teacher, tarot reader, and musical artist. Blake incorporates mystical traditions from both the East and the West with a reverence for the natural world into his own brand of spirituality. He holds a degree in English and religion from the University of Florida. He is an avid reader, knitter, crafter, pescatarian, and member of the Order of Bards, Ovates, and Druids (OBOD). He loves communing with nature and exploring its beauty, whether it is within the city or hiking in the woods. Blake lives in the New England region of the US with his beloved husband. Visit him on the web at www.blakeoctavianblair.com or write to him at blake@blakeoctavianblair.com.*

Finding Your Magical Voice

Chas Bogan

Words shape our reality. We understand much of the world through our words, and many a magician will argue that the world is in turn transformed by our words. Knowing how to speak certain charms and understanding what changes they manifest may make all the difference between summoning a powerful spirit or an odorous ferret. To help you craft your magical voice, let's take a brief look at the history of spoken-word spells, discuss some of the theories supporting the efficacy of such spells, and set you on the course to speaking with style and confidence.

For this project, I will be looking at the magical environment of North America and writing about this region's traditions with spoken-word charms (understanding that similar traditions exist throughout the world).

A highly influential book in the United States, published in 1820, is *Pow-Wows, or Long Lost Friend*, containing numerous prayers and spoken-word spells aimed at correcting various day-to-day challenges related to such concerns as healing, fire, animal husbandry,

Knowing how to speak certain charms and understanding what changes they manifest may make all the difference between summoning a powerful spirit or an odorous ferret.

and so on. This book both influenced and reflected the sort of spoken charms commonly found in the US, especially in areas such as the Ozarks and Appalachian regions. The book itself draws from various sources, notably European grimoire traditions, as well as German folk practices, some of which derive from ancient Norse religion. Let's take a moment to look at one of the spoken spells from *Pow-Wows*, this one titled "A Good Remedy to Stop Bleeding."

Say the following: "This is the day on which the injury happened. Blood, thou must stop, until the Virgin Mary brings forth another son." Repeat these words three times.

This spell has elements common to many.

The opening line, "This is the day on which the injury happened," sets up the spell, giving context and placing us at a point in time. It sacrifices poetry in its specificity. Personally, I prefer more of a balance between the two. However, in any type of spellwork, spoken or written spells particularly, it is very important to be specific. Many

stories warn about making deals with magical beings, illustrating how something in the wording could lead to one's demise, such as a person wishing for wealth being crushed by a safe full of gold. The devil is in the detail, they say, and this must be underscored when discussing spoken-word spells.

The next step of this spell issues a command: "Blood, thou must stop." Direct and to the point, this is where the spell enacts change. This, in my definition, is one difference between a prayer and a spell, in that prayer more often asks for deity to intervene in a situation, whereas a spell addresses a situation directly, demanding that it change.

The authority by which the person speaking the spell is able to command the blood to stop is granted, in this case, by its religious context. Mention of the Virgin Mary marks it as a Christian-based spell. It is important to note the rich tradition of Christian folk magic, which is the foundation of many North American traditions, such as Brauche Pow-wow, Hoodoo, Appalachian Granny Magic, and several others. Should you decide that you wish to utilize traditional spells such as this, it becomes important to consider their context. While you may not be Christian, you may still be able to connect with the legend of Mary and her not-soon-to-be-repeated virgin birth. Then again, if you feel you have been persecuted by Christianity such that you have a negative reaction to anything associated with it, then a spell with a Christian context may not work for you. We will talk more about this shortly in regard to psalms.

Another common element of the Stop Bleeding spell is the direction to repeat it three times. Numbers, as well as words, have magical associations. The number three is favored in Pow-Wow, as it engages each of the three personas of God, those being Father, Son, and Holy Spirit. Magical practitioners from different traditions may choose to repeat a spoken spell some other auspicious number of times. For inspiration, take a look at numerology or musical pitches or whatever else seems of value to you.

Let us take a look now at the tradition of reciting psalms, and how they serve as a type of spoken-word spell. The belief that the recitation of psalms can cause change in the world of God's creation is rooted in Kabala. Most individuals with a relationship to Christianity are familiar with its creation myth, which states how God spoke the universe into being. Without going too deeply into Kabalistic philosophy in this article, what is important to understand is the belief in the power of words to shape creation, recognizing that God designed the universe so that certain words are able to affect the world. Furthermore, it is believed that words within religious scripture, most notably in the book of Psalms, contain the power to cause change in the world. This belief was presented by Godfrey Selig in his book from the 1700s titled *Secrets of the Psalms*, which in the 1930s was rewritten in a nomenclature aimed at practitioners of Conjure and widely distributed throughout the United States. Beyond Selig's book, there exist today many folks who associate certain psalms with certain types of work. Sometimes their meaning is derived from the narrative of the psalm, or simply from keywords found within a psalm, such as freedom, travel, love, and so forth. The power of a given psalm may also be discovered by trial and error, and passed from worker to worker, such as by saying, "I've read this psalm each time I've gone gambling and have always walked away a winner."

Despite the rich legacy of working with psalms for magic, those who are put off by such scripture may have problems embracing the practice. I know of many magical practitioners who take their inspiration from other sources, such as literature or pop culture. The paradigm backing the power of such words is not the same as with psalms (whereby power is granted by the divine authority of Hebrew words or their translations) but can be perceived as being powerful for different reasons. For instance, poetry is often seen as being divinely inspired, such as verses inspired by the Muses of Greek mythology found in the works of Homer and Sappho. Poets of the Transcendental movement, such as Emerson and Thoreau, likewise embody the voice of nature and the sublime essence of humankind. Beyond such sacred origins, language from popular books, films, and even comic books has a unique power. While some magicians favor rarity, seeking words from obscure occult tomes or seldom-used languages such as Latin or Gaelic, others find power in sources that are well known, finding that a well-worn path is an easier route through which magic may flow than is a road less traveled. Truly, this is a matter of preference. Spoken-word spells taken from sources such as Harry Potter, *Buffy the Vampire Slayer*, *Bewitched*, or any other contemporary source have inspired magic to unfold in the minds of many, and serve as resources to inspire the same in your life.

The magician is not limited to utilizing words that have been composed by others. Magic is a form of self-expression, so crafting your own spoken charms is encouraged. Of course, not all of us are poets, and each of us has a different style and preferences. Personally, I favor spells that rhyme, but just as some of the best poetry is non-rhyming, so too are some of the best spoken spells. (Consider the Stop Bleeding spell from earlier.) Often, the spells found in literary or cinematic sources rhyme. The witches in Shakespeare's *Macbeth* might not be quite so dramatic without the anticipation of what ingredients might rhyme with the line "silver'd in the moon's eclipse." Should you choose to chant your spell numerous times, as discussed earlier, rhyming spells offer a certain ease and a melodious quality. The only thing to be aware of if you choose to craft a rhyming chant is not to get so bogged down in the rhyme that the specificity and directness of your spell is lost.

A lot can be learned by studying how affirmations are used. Affirmations are common among magicians who identify as New Age or lightworkers. The paradigm by which affirmations are often believed to work has less to do with the words themselves holding power, such as with the psalms, but draws more from Theosophical philosophy the understanding that our beliefs direct our reality. Many are familiar with the Law of Attraction, which forms the basis of books such as *The Secret*. The concept here is that your thoughts attract similar conditions; therefore, affirmations are used to train your thoughts to manifest your desired outcome. Statements like "I am loved" or "I am brave" are used to convince yourself that you possess these qualities, thus drawing to yourself more love or bravery. Rules for affirmations insist that negative statements never be used and that phrases never be put in the future tense. You would not say "I will find love," as that would reinforce the idea that you do not have love in the moment. Neither would you say "I am fearless," as a lack of fear does not equate to bravery. These same rules should apply to how you craft your spoken-word spells.

> **The concept here is that your thoughts attract similar conditions; therefore, affirmations are used to train your thoughts to manifest your desired outcome.**

Spell to Find and Strengthen Your Magical Voice

Since this article seeks to aid you in finding your magical voice through spoken-word spells, let us work now to craft a spell to do exactly that.

First, let us orient ourselves and set the foundation with the following verse:

From my chest,
my throat,
and my lips, I exhale.

Such specificity may seem overstated; however, it forms a solid tradition, similar to what we encountered with the Stop Bleeding spell. With these words, a journey has been tracked; in this instance, the journey of one's breath, which at its end orients us in the present moment.

Now comes the command:

My words make magic,
My will prevails.

A couple of things are happening with these final lines. A command is made of your words; they will make magic. As with all magic, your intention is as important as the words you use, so be sure you have a clear concept of what you are demanding. Each of your words should be analyzed so that you fully define their meaning.

To put a finer point on it, let's look at the word *magic*. What type of magic are we talking about? Personally, I'm not one to add a *k* to the end of this word in order to differentiate it from stage magic, but I understand that some folks do this since context cues alone do not always help distinguish between sleight-of-hand magic and the more metaphysical variety. But beyond that, even when we recognize that this word relates to supernatural magic, folks have different ideas about what that means. To some, magic is no more than a mood or a mindset, and to others, it's something more physically dynamic. Some see magic as a process, whereas others expect immediate and sometimes spectacular change. It is therefore important to be certain that you have a full understanding of each word you use in order to define your expectations.

For this spoken charm, I suggest repeating it three times. It should serve as a means of strengthening your confidence in the magic of your voice. This will aid you in speaking with the correct attitude, as it is important that you speak with authority and have faith in the power of your words. Even if you have never considered yourself to have a way with words, understanding that your voice is a powerful magical tool will greatly enrich your magic.

Chas Bogan (San Francisco, CA) is a professional Conjure doctor who practices at his store, the Mystic Dream. He is an initiate and practitioner of various metaphysical traditions, teaching classes on Conjure and Feri at the online school of which he is a founder, Mystic Dream Academy, as well as at conventions and festivals. He also produces talking boards (Carnivalia) and spiritual supplies steeped in Hoodoo (Modern Conjure). Find him online at ChasBogan.com.

Witchcraft Essentials

Practices, Rituals & Spells

Pocket-Size Protection Symbols

Lexa Olick

Being practically raised in Niagara Falls, where waterfalls are blasted with rainbows of light each night, I learned from an early age to see magic in nature. I went to school in Buffalo, New York, so I spent most of my days in a city so renowned for its snowstorms that the inhabitants warmly refer to them as snowmageddon, snownado, or snowzilla. The weather was unpredictable, so I was taught to expect the worst.

Of course, the worst didn't happen until I was an adult. I was a college student when a lake-effect snowstorm launched a sneak attack early in October. We called it the "October Surprise" of 2006. The weight of snow and ice sent trees crashing into power lines, cars, and houses. Students were trapped inside their dorms with no heat, light, or power. We were crammed shoulder to shoulder in complete darkness. It would be days before the power was restored.

The snow piled high against the buildings, and some students thought they could slide down the snow, like a cartoon, and land into safety. They looked around the room and decided that I was the lightest, so they graciously volunteered me to be the first one down the snow slide. I politely declined, but other students were excited to participate. I sensed it would end badly, so I grabbed my backpack, which was stuffed with sketchbooks and artist trading cards, and chucked it out the window.

The backpack didn't slide safely down the snow. It plummeted to the ground and left a distinct hole in the snow where it fell. The students then decided that fresh snow might not be the best support for the weight of a human being. Unfortunately, the students in the other dormitory missed our demonstration, and someone did end up with a broken leg.

For many freshmen, this was their first experience living away from home. They had heard stories about Buffalo snow, so many teary-eyed students had turned to me, shaking, and asked, "Is it always like this?" It took a lot of hugging and coddling to reassure them that this was not a normal fall day in Buffalo.

The snow eventually stopped, but the impact of the storm was still apparent. Thousands of trees were destroyed, making it impossible to fix the power lines. Crowded, cold, and panicked, I did what any other student wished they could do: run home to Mommy.

Family is a safe haven for most people during a disaster, so the dread of the snowstorm began to melt when I arrived back home. I finally saw light, and the snow now glistened underneath the sun. My parents lived in the country, so trees had fallen without much damage. Thanks to my father's green thumb, my parents always had a beautiful backyard. The day after the storm, I remember just staring at the mulberry tree. The branches and leaves were encased in ice. The ice was so clear that it looked like glass. Everything was still and quiet. It was as if the tree had been frozen by a snow queen to preserve its beauty forever. I felt at peace.

Snow has always comforted me. So even now, as an adult, I arrange my schedule so I spend winters close to home and the snowfall. However, last year was the first time in twenty-seven years that I didn't feel the snow on my face.

I finally gave up Buffalo snow for some sun and sand. I even bought new travel necessities, but not everything had RFID protection (which protects credit cards from being skimmed). Fortunately, RFID protection sleeves and cards are available to easily transfer from one bag to the next, so I'm always protected. The RFID protection cards remind me of the personal protection cards I make to carry. The ease of carrying wallet-size symbols allows me to go about my day with added spiritual protection.

Just as the mulberry tree quieted my thoughts after the October Surprise snowstorm, seeing a familiar symbol can calm my nerves during tense times. So I draw my favorite symbols on cards that are small enough to fit in my wallet. That way, I can carry them in my purse or slip them in my pocket whenever I change outfits. Plus, I can whip them out and pass them along to friends. I can even slip a card into a tarot deck to cleanse and protect it.

I collect tarot decks, so I like to keep them safe. I look for old decks at garage sales because I like cards with a past. I can see and feel the history in every crease. While I love the vintage tarot cards, my first-ever deck was bought new in the shrink wrap.

My first tarot deck was a little impersonal. The cards didn't call out to me. I was a child and bought what was left on the shelf. I didn't relate to the art. However, I kept the deck safe inside a box that I personalized. I used scraps of old family clothes, onto which I had screen-printed Romani protection symbols. The result was a visual patchwork of memories. So a very generic stack of cards became something special.

My tarot decks remind me of artist trading cards (ATCs), which are my favorite memory from art school. These cards weren't a homework assignment, so artists were free to express themselves any way they chose without fear of judgment. ATCs were traded among students, teachers, and local artists. The tradition was a very intimate experience, and I was honored whenever anyone wanted to trade with me.

My tarot box inspired my ATCs (artist trading cards). Scraps of cloth and paper became the canvas, and protection symbols passed on to me by family were sketched in charcoal.

My tarot box inspired my ATCs. Scraps of cloth and paper became the canvas, and protection symbols passed on to me by family were sketched in charcoal. It was another visual patchwork of memories. My peers liked the idea that ATCs could be tools of protection. ATCs were one of the few belongings I had during the October Surprise snowstorm. The cards were inside my backpack that was chucked out the window instead of me. I fondly remember the time I spent carrying ATCs, because those cards gave me confidence, inspiration, and warmth. College is a challenging stage in life, but the ATCs gave me a sense of belonging. I traded with a lot of artists that year. The artists kept my ATC on the top of their stack for protection, which is very similar to how I keep my tarot cards. My intent was to create tiny works of art to trade with others, but what came naturally to me was something magical, personal, and functional.

How to Make Your Own Pocket-Size Protection Symbols

To create your own protection cards, you will need these supplies:

- Precut cards, such as blank business cards or unlined index cards (optional)

- 8.5 x 11–inch sheet of card stock (optional)

- 3.5 x 2–inch wooden business cards (optional)

- A photograph with a blank reverse side (optional)

- Scissors

- A ballpoint pen

- Colored pencils (optional)

STEP ONE

You can use precut cards, such as blank business cards or unlined index cards, or you can cut the cards yourself from an 8.5 x 11 sheet of card stock. The standard size of a tarot card is 2.75 x 4.75 inches, wallet-size is 2.5 x 3.5 inches, and business cards are generally 3.5 x 2 inches. If in doubt, you can always use your own business card, reward card, photograph, or tarot card as a stencil. Use any paper you feel comfortable drawing on, but I recommend card stock because it's thicker than most paper. I especially like the look of drawings on wood, so I suggest using blank wooden business cards if you want the strongest material. You can also use a photograph if the back of it is blank. Trim your paper to the desired size.

Step Two

Using a ballpoint pen, draw your symbol in the center of the paper. Use a symbol that speaks to you. The hamsa symbol (a hand with an eye in the center) wards off negative energy. The yin-yang symbol represents balance. Pentagrams represent all the elements that make up life and the nature of humankind. Spirals symbolize life, evolution, and growth. Use any image that communicates meaning to you. You can use traditional protection symbols or any image that personally invokes a feeling of security or love. Think of an object or shape that you feel a connection to, whether it's a flower, an animal, the moon, or a crystal. When you draw the image on your paper, the paper becomes a bearer of power.

Step Three

I like the simple and traditional look of a line drawing, but you can fill the symbol with color if you desire. Use colored pencils and fill in the empty spaces. Choose colors that represent your symbol or the feelings you wish to convey when you look at your drawing.

Keep your symbol close to you by carrying it in your bag, pocket, or wallet. Keep objects safe by placing the card in your books or tarot deck. You can always keep the card with you to feel protected, or hold it in your hands to channel the meaning behind your symbol.

Lexa Olick *is the author of* Witchy Crafts: 60 Enchanted Projects for the Creative Witch *and has contributed to many of the Llewellyn annuals. She is a graduate of the University of Buffalo, where she studied art and art history. Her artistic journey began as a web designer, but her true passions lie in jewelry design and doll making. When she is not writing or crafting, she spends her free time traveling, gardening, and adding to her collection of antique glassware. She currently lives in New York with her family and several hyperactive pets.*

Pagan Prayer Beads

Autumn Damiana

L ike many other Pagans I know, I was
once a Catholic. And while Catholi-
cism no longer calls to me, there are still
aspects of it that I treasure and miss, like
the ritual and tactile experience of praying the rosary. When I became a Pagan,
I wondered how I could hold on to this
sacred mystery in a way that matched
my newfound faith. I read up on the rosary and other types of prayer beads, and
I discovered that there is no established
tradition in Paganism for their construction or use. This means that there are no
rules either, and that we are free to make
our own!

Prayer Bead History

In Western culture, the rosary is the most easily recognized type of prayer bead, but it is not the oldest. Prayer beads have been around for millennia and most likely originated in India with Hindu malas. These were borrowed by Buddhist monks, who in turn introduced the beads to Christianity and Islam. Each culture has developed their own prayer bead traditions, such as the number of beads used.

A Catholic rosary, for example, has 59 beads, while the Islamic misbaha (or tasbih) has 100 beads, and the japa malas in use by Hindus and Buddhists have 108 beads. To signify which prayer to say next or when to repeat prayers, beads may be grouped into sections. Eastern Orthodox Christians don't use beads at all, but rather make a "prayer rope" consisting of knots. Greeks also sometimes use "worry beads" that have no religious meaning but are simply for fidgeting with to relax and help pass the time.

Most prayer beads have a circular structure, but there are variations. The rosary has a center medal trailing five beads and a cross. Malas are circlets with a large tassel attached, often worn as necklaces or bracelets. Islamic prayer beads can have string, beads, or tassels dangling from them. Noncircular prayer bead strands are not as traditional but are becoming more and more common, especially through alternative religions like Paganism.

Constructing Prayer Beads

Making a set of prayer beads is as easy as stringing beads on a cord, sometimes with knots in between. Beads can be made of stone, glass, metal, ceramic/clay, wood, horn, bone, shell, or even paper. While paper beads may not hold up as well over time, interesting things can be done with the paper if you are making the beads yourself. Above all, avoid using plastic (including metalized plastic), because something as sacred as a set of prayer beads should be made of natural substances. You don't need to spend a lot to make your strand, but use the nicest materials you can reasonably afford, like ceramic or stone. You may also want to include "spacer" beads, which are usually made of inexpensive glass or metal and are used to help space out your larger and more expensive beads along a string. For cord, try embroidery thread, waxed cotton or linen, hemp, jute, leather, or yarn. Again, use only natural cording materials. Make sure that the cord you pick will fit through the holes in the beads you are using! You don't have to use spacers or knots between each bead, but if you do, the beads will be easier to grasp and the strand will feel nicer as it slips through your fingers.

Something as sacred as a set of prayer beads should be made of natural substances....Use the nicest materials you can reasonably afford, like ceramic or stone.

Ideas for Prayer Bead Crafts

One of the least expensive and most meaningful ways to create your own prayer beads is to recycle. Maybe you have bead jewelry that broke or that belonged to a relative, a pendant that you never wear, or a bead craft that your child made at school (in this case, plastic beads are okay). These would all be perfect to reuse in making your prayer beads, both to benefit from their inherent positive energies and to give them new life, honoring the earth by keeping them out of a landfill. You can also recycle beads you buy secondhand. Just make sure to energetically clear/cleanse these before using. The easiest way to do this is to smudge the beads with a cleansing herb such as sage or cedar, or perform whatever cleansing ritual you do on your altar tools.

Here are some other bead types, charm ideas, and correspondences to consider when making prayer beads.

FOUR ELEMENTS

Fire: Red or orange, lava, metal, pyrite, garnet, tiger's eye, fire-polished glass, sun, star, lightning bolt, salamander/dragon

Water: Blue, shell, frosted glass, real or glass pearls, coral, calcite, sea life, goblet, teardrop, cloud

Earth: Green or brown, wood, ceramic/clay, seeds, bone/horn, agate, jasper, leaf, tree, globe, forest animals

Air: Yellow or white, paper, clear glass, citrine, selenite, fluorite, birds, flying insects, feather, hot air balloon, swirl/spiral

GODDESS AND GOD

Goddess: Silver, moon, shell, cauldron, bee, apple, rose

God: Gold, sun, antler, sword, arrow, crown, oak leaf

Triple Goddess colors: White (maiden), red (mother), black (crone)

Triple God colors: Green (youth), yellow (warrior), brown (sage)

NUMERICAL CORRESPONDENCES

Any meaningful number can be used in individual bead sections or for the total number of beads. Here are some ideas:

- 13 (full moons in a year)

- 21 (13 moons + 8 sabbats in a year)

- 27 (which is 3 x 3 x 3, a good spell number)

- 28 (days in a moon cycle)

• Add up your birth date—e.g., Dec. 17, 1979 = 12 (Dec.) + 8 (1 + 7) + 26 (1 +9 +7 +9) = 3 + 8 + 26 = 37. Or reduce even further: 3 + 7 = 10, good for a short strand or bead section.

Longer strands can include spacer beads to boost the count. For example, you could use 366 beads to symbolize the Wiccan year and a day.

Making Your Own Beads

This is a lot of fun and much easier than you might think!

Paper Beads

Search the internet for online tutorials on how to make these. You can write charms or verses on the inside of the beads before rolling them up, or print out an appropriate text on decorative paper to cut up and make your beads. You can also infuse the paper with scent. Try brushing on very small amounts of essential oils with a cotton swab, spritzing on scented water, or holding the paper over incense smoke for a few minutes.

Clay Beads

Choose natural air-dry clay and stay away from polymer clay, because the latter is basically plastic. Air-dry clay comes in a variety of colors, but once dry, the clay can also be painted. Simply roll a ball of clay into the desired shape, poke a hole through it with a needle or toothpick, and let it dry. Then paint or decorate it as you like.

Wood Beads

There are a few options here. One is to find a length of branch or a dowel around ½ to 1 inch in diameter and cut it into pieces with a craft saw, then use a pin vise to drill holes in each piece. You can add additional decoration, such as paint, stain, or wood-burned designs. Another

idea is to save pits from stone fruits, like cherries or apricots. Use a pair of pliers to hold the pit while you scrub away all remnants of the fruit with a stiff brush and then drill a hole using the pin vise. Watermelon, pumpkin, or gourd seeds pierced with a needle can also be used as beads or spacers.

Writing and Using Prayers

Prayers can be petitions or words of worship, but they can also be chants, meditation exercise`s, or even spells. Your prayers should be short and easy to remember, and they don't have to rhyme unless you want them to. Don't be afraid to use what you already know. Chants, poems, spells, and well-known Pagan verses (like the Charge of the Goddess or the Witches' Mill) are suitable to use as prayers. Remember that each short prayer or each line from a longer prayer corresponds to a bead, a section of beads, or a charm, so you might want to write or structure your prayer at the same time that you make your bead strand, adjusting as necessary. Simple text is sometimes the most effective, such as "Fall seven times, stand up eight" (Japanese proverb), "May your troubles be less, and your blessings be more, and nothing but happiness come through your door" (Irish blessing), or a saying that I often use: "Goddess, show me my path, that I may walk in your ways."

Prayers can be petitions or words of worship, but they can also be chants, meditation exercises, or even spells. Your prayers should be short and easy to remember, and they don't have to rhyme unless you want them to.

Chakra Meditation Beads

This short strand of beads will help you open and cleanse your chakras. By repeating the mantra associated with each chakra, you are in effect producing a sound healing. Chanting the mantras while using your beads will also bring on a meditative state. Gather these materials:

- 1 foot of hemp string

- 7 beads in rainbow colors that correspond to the seven chakras (see below). Select large beads with holes big enough to string on the hemp cording. Glass, ceramic, wood, or gemstones are all good choices.

- A vial of glass E-beads in a neutral color

Simply string your beads in rainbow order on the hemp, using three E-beads as spacers in between. Knot the hemp at each end, next to the beginning bead and the end bead. To pray, concentrate on the chakra's location in your body as you hold each bead. Say the mantra that is appropriate for each chakra and color:

LAM (red, root chakra)

VAM (orange, sacral chakra)

RAM (yellow, solar plexus chakra)

YAM (green, heart chakra)

HAM (blue, throat chakra)

OM (indigo or purple, third eye chakra)

AH (purple or white, crown chakra)

See YouTube for videos on pronunciation, tone, and meditative music to go with your mantra chanting.

Prayer Beads of Gratitude

So many prayers are of the "asking" variety, where we pray for what we need and want. Yet it is equally important to thank deity for both our prayers answered and the blessings we already have. These prayer beads will help you do just that, and each use will be a different experience.

Gather these materials:

- 1–2 yards of waxed cotton or linen cord

- 1 focal charm (sun, moon, pentacle, ankh, Celtic knot, etc.)

- 28 eye-catching and/or meaningful beads of your choice

Fold your cording in half, and use it to make a lark's head knot through the loop of your charm. This will anchor the charm in place and leave two long tails. Starting with one tail, make an overhand knot in the cord close to the charm. Then string on a bead and make another knot. Continue this pattern for fourteen of your beads. Then repeat on the other tail with the other fourteen beads. Finally, tie the two tails together and trim.

To pray, start with your charm and say the following:

Favored I am by the Goddess [or insert another deity here] above, bestowed with fortune, blessings, and love. My gratitude I give you in honor of _____.

State one thing you are grateful for with each bead, always ending with these words:

For this, O Goddess (or other deity), hear my prayer of thanks.

Here is an example:

> ...*My gratitude I give you in honor of finding a new job closer to home.*
> *For this, O Demeter, hear my prayer of thanks.*

You can state anything at all that you are grateful for, big or small, or you can simply repeat the same blessing with each bead as a mantra or meditation.

If your circlet of prayer beads is long enough, you can tie the end of each tail to a barrel clasp so you can wear the beads like a necklace! If this is your goal, find beads to use that are big/long enough, or use spacer beads instead of knots to lengthen the strand.

Free-Form Prayer Beads

The sky is the limit with these types of prayer beads. You can divide a circlet into four sections to represent the elements/cardinal directions, and use it as a kind of pocket-size altar. Or string a strand with beads and charms of personal significance to you and write prayers of self-blessing or grounding/centering to go along with them. A circlet or strand does not need to be symmetrical, nor does it need to be long—you can string a bracelet on elastic thread, or use a bit of strong cording and make a key chain. With a little research, some crafty know-how, and a good imagination, you too can make Pagan prayer beads that are beautiful, functional, portable, and, above all, meaningful.

Autumn Damiana *is an author, artist, crafter, and amateur photographer. She is a solitary eclectic Cottage Witch who has been following her Pagan path for almost two decades and is a regular contributor to the Llewellyn annuals. Along with writing and making art, Autumn has a degree in early childhood education and is currently pursuing further studies. She lives with her husband and doggie familiar in the beautiful San Francisco Bay Area. Visit her online at autumndamiana.com.*

Travel-Size Altars

Ash W. Everell

For the witch who's constantly on the go, a full ceremonial altar kit with all the bells and whistles may not be a feasible (or even applicable) thing to take on the road. When traveling for business, backpacking around, or simply going on a holiday, a travel altar is a wonderfully portable way to take your specific practice with you, wherever you may go.

Finding the Perfect Box

The key to assembling the ideal mobile altar is finding the perfect container for it. A box that latches or otherwise snaps shut is the perfect vessel. If you'd like a

fancier type, you can find tons of small decorative boxes that safely close while rattling around in a purse, backpack, or pocket. If you're more of a DIY sort, an Altoids or candy tin is the best place to start. Here are some examples of boxes you might have lying around that make perfect starter boxes:

- A metal box for mints or candies (like an Altoids box)
- A sewing kit box
- A cookie tin
- A clutch purse or small wallet
- A jewelry box
- A shoebox
- A lidded jar (You can use the inside of the lid for your altar table or pentacle!)

You can customize your box to match your distinct path, style, and traditions. Paint can be used to cover the interior of the box as an all-over wallpaper to set the tone for your portable altar, or you can paint a representation of your patron deity, an image of the night sky with prominent planets and stars, or even a very literal image of your real or ideal temple setting. The bottom half of the box can be painted or decorated with patterns traditionally associated with altar cloths, embellished with a built-in pentacle, or marked with placements for your tools. Once you're happy with your setup, you can put a coat of enamel or varnish over the paint, or leave it unfinished so you can paint over it time and time again afterward.

If the texture of paint doesn't feel right for your altar interior, get creative! Contact paper and wallpaper samples are available, sometimes for free, at many hardware and home improvement stores. You can find scraps of luxurious velvet and satin fabric, and gently glue them into place inside the box. You can even add straps and ribbons to hold your items in place when they're inside your mobile altar.

What Goes Inside

Your travel altar should be a reflection of your everyday altar. In other words, it should contain everything you regularly need when you engage in your witchcraft practice. For me, that means a candle, a wand, some incense, and a vial of something to offer. For you, this likely varies to a great extent.

Start by looking at your regular altar or commonly used tools. If you don't have a regular altar you use, start by making a list of the tools you use most in your witchcraft. Then go down the list and mark your essentials—anything you can't do magick without. Once you've got your core tools, you can start to find portable versions of those tools to stock your new magical cabinet. Here are some common tools used in modern witchcraft and some ideas on how to safely store small versions of them in your travel altar.

CANDLES

Many witches use a candle or two as their altar centerpiece. A tealight candle is a perfect replacement for a central altar candle, and two spell or chime candles fit nicely into a mints box or cigarette case if you require two candles to represent notions like the sun and moon or the God and Goddess. You can preload your candles for their representational purposes by dressing them for their devotional purposes just as you would for spell preparation (with runes, color, oils, herbs, etc.). For example, I'd carry a tealight candle scented with jasmine and camphor for a travel altar to the Lady Moon.

INCENSE

Cone incense is absolutely perfect for use in a travel altar. A lot of cone incense in packets comes with its own fire-safe metal disc on which to burn incense, which you can pop right into your travel altar, along with a piece of cone incense that corresponds to your purpose. Cone incense tends to last only for about twenty minutes, so you might want to keep a supply on hand to reload your altar when necessary. If you don't have one of these little metal discs on hand, not to worry! Cone incense fits perfectly onto an American quarter or a British pound coin. Using a coin doubles as a correspondence as well, with an extra boost of luck and communication and a nod to Hermes.

LIGHTER OR MATCHES

Neither of the previous tools would be of any use without this one, would they? A flat book of matches should fit neatly into your box without taking up too much space, whereas a full-size lighter might be a bit too much. Of course, many gas stations do sell half-size lighters, but the environmentally conscious witch can rely on matches.

STONES

A small tumbled stone for meditation, grounding, or providing a sense of space, or even a rounded one for divination, would be a great choice to keep in your travel altar. Regardless of how frequently you use stones in your regular altar, keeping a stone in your travel altar might be a good idea, as it can provide a sense of grounding and also be a way for you to carry a little piece of the ground from home with you when you travel.

Small Glass Vials

Those little glass corked vials that you can find at craft stores are perfect for storing premixed blessed water, rainwater, salt water, or anything in between. You can usually fit one or two vials in a mints tin. To prepare for travel, perform any ritual to bless or consecrate your water before you leave. Be sure to label the vials so you know what's in them!

Salt

This can be held in a small pouch or, in the case of the exceptionally thrifty witch, in a single-use packet from a restaurant or gas station. Use it on the go for purifying purposes, to prepare holy water, and for any other salt-based witchcraft activities. If you carry water in your glass vial, you'll be able to create blessed water during ritual on the go.

Wand

Believe it or not, you can probably fit a small wand in your box. Twigs make lovely natural wands, and many modern wandmakers even make miniature or portable wands precisely for this purpose.

Deity Representations

If you work with deities or powers, you can carry a portable representation of them in your travel altar. I personally like pasting an image or a picture of my patron deity onto the upper lid of the box so she's propped up when the lid is open. You might like to paint, apply, or insert a representation of your deities or powers, or include a small token representative of them—a dried rosebud for Aphrodite or dice for Hermes, for example. The representation could be included inside the box or painted on the inside lid or cover. That way, the image won't get dinged up or damaged, and you can easily keep your sacred space sacred (even though it's the size of a mints tin).

PENTACLE

For witches who use this altar element, you can actually bake it right into the structure of your altar! Using paint or sacred ink, you can draw a working pentacle on the bottom, or "floor," of your altar too, or you can carve one. For witches who prefer the traditional idea of a pentacle disc, you can find or create small versions of the tool yourself. Here are some ideas:

- Weave small willow twigs, using string to secure them, for a wooden pentacle.

- Take a coin, perhaps a large and exotic one, and paint or draw your pentacle on it.

- Cut or shave down a piece of tree bark to form a proper pentacle circle.

- Form clay or sand dough into the shape of a pentacle and bake.

- Mold warm wax into a circle and carve your pentacle into it with a pin or needle.

Traveling with Your Altar

When traveling by plane with your altar, you should be aware of the current air travel regulations. As a witch who's accidentally left my athame in my suitcase, I can attest to the importance of assembling a travel-safe altar when traveling by air (in order to avoid a lengthy and awkward explanation of witchcraft to the TSA!).

Always place your travel altar in your checked luggage, unless it contains an item prohibited in checked luggage. It can be tempting to want to have constant access to your travel altar, but certain items can't be placed in your carry-on—matches, flammables, and sharp objects being some of them. Most people's altars, of course, generally contain all three of these things and thus are probably best relegated to checked luggage. Certain countries actually outlaw the use and import of witchcraft and witch's tools, so do your research when traveling internationally and try not to break any laws.

Certain countries actually outlaw the use and import of witchcraft and witch's tools, so do your research when traveling internationally.

Here are some common witchcraft items that are fine on the ground but are prohibited in the air:

- **Athames and knives:** This seems obvious, but pen knives and Swiss army knives count too!

- **Large liquid vials:** Keeping it under 3.4 ounces per vial is the key.

- **Flammables:** I've been okay carrying a lighter, but incense, matches, or highly flammable items might be a problem.

All of these things can be carried in your checked luggage, however, so it's probably best to tuck your travel altar in your checked suitcase.

When traveling by train, boat, or car, it's much simpler because you can, of course, retain full ownership of your travel altar throughout the journey. A word of warning, however: if you're traveling in the summer and you leave your altar unattended in the heat, your candles will almost certainly melt and be damaged. It's best to keep your altar out of the heat, perhaps in your bag or a drawer or in the shade—not in a parked car in the Southwest in August!

You'll also probably want to check regularly to see if your travel altar needs replenishing. Only so many candles, vials, and so on can fit in such a small space, so ensure you're always prepared by checking to see what you need every time you return from your travels.

Consecrating Your Altar

You may want to wrap a string, cord, ribbon, or rubber band around your portable altar box when you take it on the go. That way, its contents won't spill all over your pocket or purse. It's also important to properly prepare, bless, and consecrate your altar so it can be your magical work table wherever you go, as well as be cleansed of its previous energies. Such a string (or ribbon or band) can be incorporated into a simple altar consecration ritual. You will need the following:

- A length of black string (or cord or ribbon or a rubber band) or a string in a color you personally associate with your own craft

- A white candle (in a holder)

- Salt and water

Clean your altar box. Some boxes can be cleansed just by dunking them in blessed water (mix your salt and water here) and drying with a cloth, but wooden boxes and certain metal boxes should not be exposed to water. In these cases, you may want to give the box a thorough dry dusting and asperge it with some incense or cleansing smoke.

Lay the string down and place your closed travel altar upon it. Put your candle near your cord and altar arrangement.

Take a moment to ground and center yourself. When you're ready, light the candle and say a blessing over your travel altar. You can use the following blessing, or alter (no pun intended!) it to suit your purpose:

Bless this altar, come with me,
In my bag, safe you'll be.

When the altar is blessed, seal the magic by tying the string tightly around it. I like to use a bow with three knots for extra trifold magic. Then blow out the candle.

Next time you use your altar, you can "open" and "close" your ritual state by opening and closing your knotted cord. (For those who don't have time to fiddle with ribbons, rubber bands do come in a lot of corresponding colors!)

You can also use the four elements—earth, air, fire, and water—to add the traditional consecration elements to the ritual. Simply expose the altar to each element (perhaps dirt for earth, incense for air, flame for fire, and holy water or moon water for water), say the blessing, and finish the ritual.

A Little Piece of Home

Remember, the whole point of a travel altar is to keep a piece of your own personal witchcraft space with you. As long as you tailor your travel altar to your tastes and include the tools you use the most, you'll be able to enjoy your altar away from home for years to come!

Ash W. Everell *is a practicing Green Witch of four years, currently located somewhere deep in the woods of Vermont. They run the popular witching blog* Theory of Magick *(http://theoryofmagick.tumblr.com), and when they're not casting or doing magical research, they enjoy collecting vinyl records, drag culture, and spending time with their partner and cat (both mischievous!).*

Online Research
for Pagan Writers

Susan Pesznecker

As a Pagan living in today's digital age, you're likely spending more time writing than you ever imagined. Perhaps you've created a blog or agreed to publish a newsletter or organize training materials for a grove, coven, or other group. You may be writing a book or zine for publication. Or you might just want to craft a pithy reply to someone's social media post—backed up by strong evidence.

One thing's certain: you've realized how important it is to support your work with strong, reliable source materials. But you probably wonder if you could be doing it better. Is there an easier way to do research and locate the best resources, especially beyond simply using Google?

Yes. Yes, there is.

I'm going to give you some ways to find strong source materials, use them correctly, and do this efficiently—because any chance to save time is a plus, right?

Let's dig in!

When Should You Use Source Materials in Your Writing?

For the most part, your writing should be in your own voice. People who read your writing want to know what you have to say, not to see you summarize other people's work. But if you need more information about a topic, are trying to support a controversial position, or want to bring evidence into the work, you may need to use sources. Choose the best ones possible and don't let them overpower your own ideas.

Where Can You Find Good Source Materials Online?

The "free web"—public browsers and search engines—is a great source of information. Unfortunately, it's also a fabulous source of crap, if you'll excuse the expression. Knowing how to cut through the crap will make your searches easier and more productive and will leave you with stronger results.

Let's look at Google, the resource used by most people. When using Google, consider the following:

- First, many of Google's top search results are there *not* because they're the most popular but because someone has paid big money to make sure their results stay in the top two or three pages of the results list. Thus, you may need to dig through a few pages to start seeing useful results.

- Second, all search engines use "filter bubbles." Simply put, they use algorithms—combined with whatever they know about you—to predict the results you want to see, and then they provide those results. This means you may have trouble finding materials that disagree with what you already know. If this happens, vary your search terms and try some advanced search techniques. (Read on!)

- Third, use one- or two-word search terms, as shorter search strings yield more focused results. For example, try "wand wood energy" instead of "what kind of wood makes wands with the strongest energy?" Use singular rather than plural terms.

What Do We Even Mean by "Good" Source Materials?

Screen your sources with the CRAP test, a test widely used by college libraries in the US to evaluate currency, reliability, authority, and purpose. A quick Google search for "CRAP Test" will give you more details. Also:

- Look for sources written by experts: those with traditional college degrees or work or life experience in the subject. Many Pagan groups and traditions award "master's" and doctorate" degrees that, although important in that tradition, aren't comparable to the same degrees in a university setting. This may be a plus or a minus in your search, so just be aware of it.

- Check the date of the source. If you're writing about a recent topic, you'll want the newest sources. If you're writing about a more classic topic, older historical sources may work too.

- Consider the domain name in the URL address. Dot-com sites are commercial or personal, often include advertisements, and may be less authoritative. Dot-org sites may be personal or owned by nonprofits. Dot-gov and .edu sites are run by the government and educational institutions, respectively, and are almost always reliable.

- Look for a professional-appearing site with few or no advertisements and carefully proofed, unbiased language. These findings suggest the author is more interested in sharing information than selling products.

- The best sites provide contact information as well as information about the authors. When an author is interested in having an intellectual discussion, they're also interested in letting you know who they are, their background, and so forth.

Is Wikipedia a Reliable Source?

That's an interesting question. Wikipedia is not regarded as authoritative by people in academia. Why? Because Wiki entries can be written and edited by anyone, including people with no expertise in a topic. This violates the academic position of preferring source material to be written by experts. That said, many Wiki articles contain good, carefully sourced material, and most have useful lists of sources at the bottom of the web page. Use Wikipedia to inform yourself about a topic, then look for stronger sources to actually use.

How Can You Find Strong, Free Web Sources Without Scrolling Through Pages of Dreck?

Using advanced search techniques will help you sift through the rubbish and get right to the good stuff. These techniques will help you "Google like a librarian":

- Use quotation marks around the search terms to return results with the search terms in that order. **"Echinacea tincture"** could return "Creating Echinacea Tinctures" but would not return "Creating a Tincture of Echinacea."

- Use a capitalized **AND** (without quotation marks) between search terms to include both terms in any order in the search results. **Echinacea AND tincture** could return "Creating Echinacea Tinctures" or "Creating a Tincture of Echinacea."

- Use a capitalized **OR** (no quotation marks) between terms to include one or the other in search results. **Echinacea OR tincture** could return "Creating Echinacea Tinctures," "Growing Echinacea in Your Yard," or "How to Make a Hot Water Echinacea Tincture."

- Precede search terms with **site:.domain** to return results from a preferred URL domain. For example, **site:.edu "echinacea tincture"** would return results from educational websites.

- Precede search terms with **intitle:** to return results that include the terms in the page title. For example, **intitle: "echinacea tincture"** would return websites with "Echinacea Tincture" in the title of the web page.

- Precede search terms with a hyphen/minus to exclude a word from search results. For example, **"echinacea tincture" -alcohol** would return results about echinacea tinctures but without the word "alcohol" appearing in the article.

- Follow search terms with **filetype:** to limit your search to a specific type of file (instead of just html). For example, **"echinacea tincture" filetype:pdf** would return results that are available in PDF form—which is handy!

- You can also combine several of these at once, like this: **site:.edu "echinacea tincture" filetype:pdf.**

What about Using "Canned Quotes" in Your Writing?

As a rule, avoid sites that gather quotations. They're often inaccurate, leading to widespread dissemination of fake quotes. Ideally, find an original source for every quotation you use. Wikiquote provides sources for all quotes, and Google Books are a great resource for original source material. If you must use a quotation, it should *perfectly* match your subject and context. Don't quote Aristotle when you're talking about the many uses of calendula!

Where Are Some Academic Collections You Can Tap Into at No Cost?

Searching for "Google Books" will take you to the Google Books area, where books are freely available in whole, partial, or snippet form. One drawback is that many of the books available in full text on Google Books aren't recent—although sometimes that's a plus if you're researching a historical or arcane topic.

Searching for "Google Scholar" will take you to the Google Scholar area, giving you free access to a wide array of academic publications—those done by folks with university degrees and experience. This can be a goldmine for certain subjects. Both Google Scholar and Google Books provide a number of searching tools.

You may also want to search for open educational resources (OERs). These represent a national trend to make textbooks and materials open to free use for all. If using Google, search "Open Education Resources" with your search term on the end, e.g., **Open Educational Resources Druid**. Searching for "free textbooks" or for "free ebooks" online can also be fruitful. An important ethical note: many unscrupulous people are known to photocopy written materials or even whole books and then make them available "for free" on websites, torrent sites, social media pages, etc. This is, in fact, a kind of theft. These people are stealing intellectual property and often wages or royalties from the authors of the materials. This is flat-out wrong, and I urge you not only to avoid these sites but also to spread the word if you find one.

An important ethical note: many unscrupulous people are known to photocopy written materials or even whole books and then make them available "for free" on websites, torrent sites, social media pages, etc. This is, in fact, a kind of theft.

What Are Some Special Tricks for Finding Specifically Pagan Resources?

That's hard to answer because so much depends on your subject. Use the techniques we've covered here to look for general resources in your focus area. Join a face-to-face or online group and ask those people for recommendations. If you have college library access, use it and its librarians. Don't have this? Maybe a friend does.

How Do I Find a Nugget of Information in a Looonnnng Web Page?

You've found a perfect web source on your topic, but it goes on and on. How do you find the one sentence you need? Simple: use your computer's search function, usually COMMAND-F. Voila!

By the way, if possible, do your writing and source work with a desktop, laptop, or tablet. Trying to do good writing and research on a tiny smartphone screen is possible, but it's a little like trying to cook Thanksgiving dinner on a backpacking stove. Don't have one of these? Most public and university libraries allow the public to use their computers. When done, email the document to yourself.

What's a Better Resource: an e-Book, a Web Page, or a Periodical?

An authoritative book—whether e-book or hard copy—can be useful and satisfying to read. The drawback with books is that they immediately begin to go out of print the moment they're published. Depending on the book and your topic, this may or may not matter.

Periodicals—anything printed or published periodically—are the most reliable resources, as they're constantly updated. Examples include newspapers, magazines, and journals.

Web pages are used to store content over time as well as to create and publish new information. Remember to use your CRAP Test carefully!

What about Fact-Checking?

Many specialized websites exist to help you check the accuracy of news stories and claims—especially when they sound wacky. Do a Google search for fact-checking sites, and you'll find them. Two of the best are Snopes and PolitiFact.

What Is Plagiarism?

Intellectual property is anything that is conceptualized or created by a person: writing, art, music, or anything that had its origins within their brain. If you use someone else's intellectual property without giving them credit, you're committing plagiarism. Plagiarism is a type of dishonesty and a type of intellectual theft, and as Pagans, we need to avoid it at all costs.

Plagiarism is a type of dishonesty and a type of intellectual theft, and as Pagans, we need to avoid it at all costs.

How Do I Avoid Plagiarism?

When creating your own intellectual property, do your own unique work. If you use source materials in your own work, you must give complete credit to the material's owner. If you don't, the source material will appear to be yours—but since it isn't, that's plagiarism. And that's bad. When using source materials, follow these two steps for *each* use:

1. Acknowledge the source's author right there in the text— *immediately* after the sentences including their work. In CMS (Chicago Manual of Style) style, this is called an *in-text citation*. Imagine the author's name is Robin Blake, and you've used their 2017 work on the science of levitation (which you've also included in your list of sources at the end of your article— see step 2). Following the sentence you're using, put the author's name and the year of publication of their work in parentheses, like this:

   Recent studies have revealed that levitation can be achieved through the use of quantum magnetics (Blake 2017).

This shows the reader that the sentence's material comes from Blake's 2017 work, and this keeps you free and clear of plagiarism.

2. At the end of the article, create a list of sources. Follow one of the accepted styles, such as the following:

- CMS (Chicago Manual of Style)—Used in book publishing
- AP (Associated Press)—Used in news writing and journalism
- MLA (Modern Language Association)—Used in academics

The Purdue Online Writing Lab (see list of resources) has detailed formatting and style guides for all three of these styles.

. . . .

Using these tips should improve your research. And as with anything, practice makes perfect!

Resources

Babin, Monique, Carol Burnell, Susan Pesznecker, Nicole Rosevear, and Jaime Wood. *The Word on College Reading and Writing*. Open Oregon Educational Resources, 2017. https://openoregon.pressbooks.pub/wrd/.

Harvard Library. "Fake News, Misinformation, and Propaganda." Last updated March 28, 2017. https://guides.library.harvard.edu/fake.

Pesznecker, Susan. *Crafting Magick with Pen and Ink: Learn to Write Stories, Spells, and Other Magickal Works*. Woodbury, MN: Llewellyn, 2009.

Purdue University. "Purdue Online Writing Lab (OWL)." 1995–2018. https://owl.purdue.edu/owl/purdue_owl.html.

Susan Pesznecker is a mother, writer, nurse, college English professor, and Baden-Powell Service Association scout and lives in the beautiful Pacific Northwest with her poodles. An initiated Druid, green magick devotee, and amateur herbalist, Sue loves reading, writing, cooking, travel, camping, swimming, stargazing, and anything having to do with the outdoors. Her previous books include Crafting Magick with Pen and Ink, The Magickal Retreat: Making Time for Solitude, Intention & Rejuvenation, and Yule: Rituals, Recipes & Lore for the Winter Solstice, and she's a regular contributor to the Llewellyn annuals. Follow her at https://www.facebook.com/SusanMoonwriterPesznecker/ and on Instagram as Susan Pesznecker.

Magical Prep for the Nursery

Emyme

In my experience, every follower of an earth-based belief system (EBBS) has a specialty. I light candles; I honor the elements, the directions, and the Lady during my walks; and I write short, easy-to-perform spells. My daughter has an affinity for essential oils and crystals.

When my daughter became pregnant with her first child, it was important to incorporate certain earth-based rituals and potions into the before, during, and after periods of the birth of my granddaughter, Aurora. What follows are some of the ways we incorporated magic into the blessed event, to inspire your own ideas.

Before the Birth

With any spell, any request, or any display of gratitude, the most important and the very first item of business is a positive intention. From the start, my daughter and son-in-law set the intention to welcome a healthy child, all the while maintaining positive thoughts and energy. During her entire pregnancy, but especially in the early stages, they read books, listened to podcasts, consulted the internet, and conferred with friends and coworkers who had children. Taking what they thought were the best of those ideas, they formed a plan. They refused to show a preference for a boy or a girl, to the point of using gender-neutral pronouns. When they did learn the gender, they did not share that with the family until six weeks prior to the birth, at the baby shower.

In keeping with this gender-neutral premise, the theme of the baby shower was the honoring of and adventure in nature, specifically woodland animals, mountains, and trees. At the time, we were fortunate that there were loads of adventure-themed items available, from invitations and decorations to baby clothing. This adventure theme continues to be prominent in Aurora's clothing and toys.

One important way my daughter honors the earth is by wearing recycled clothing. She is not a fan of "fast fashion," preferring to purchase most of her clothing from thrift and consignment shops. Several of her friends gave her bags and bags of baby clothes and other items. Aurora began life with many articles of clothing, which came in handy once daycare began. Anything unused was taken to a baby and child consignment shop. In order to negate any residual energy, every article of clothing was washed in a laundry-detergent "potion" gleaned from the DIY website *Dwelling in Happiness*, which my daughter continues to

use. Here are the supplies you will need. See the website for complete instructions on how to make this detergent (http://www.dwellingin happiness.com/chemical-free-liquid-laundry-detergent/).

CHEMICAL-FREE LIQUID LAUNDRY DETERGENT

- A two-gallon or larger bucket/container

- 2 gallons water of choice

- ½ cup Arm & Hammer Super Washing Soda

- ½ cup baking soda

- ¾ cup Castile soap (Dr. Bronner's is a good choice)

- 30 drops of your favorite essential oils

- A large wooden (or plastic) spoon to stir

- 2 one-gallon glass containers

The décor in Aurora's nursery is also gender-neutral, with a color scheme of teal, yellow, and white. A large wall is covered in stars to call down celestial power and honor the heavens. Sage smudging was performed after fresh paint and carpet cleaning and before the furniture was moved in. One item, a large bureau, had been used by myself and my daughter for about ten years. That piece was thoroughly cleansed and painted to give it a new life. After all the furniture was assembled and placed, another cleansing ritual was performed with all-natural cleaning products, simply to remove actual dust and dirt from packing materials (disposed of in an earth-friendly way). This also served to remove any less-than-positive energies attached to those who assisted in the assembling and setup of the room.

Here are instructions on how to make your own cleansing spray. This is also great to use as a quick, safe fruit and veggie wash. Rinse well after cleansing.

ALL-NATURAL CLEANING/CLEANSING POTION

- 10 drops lemon essential oil added to no more than 10 ounces water of your choice

- Spray bottle

Car seats were also thoroughly cleansed. Anything that could not be cleansed through wet washing or sage smudging was cleansed through the simple spell/act of intention of the laying on of hands, and whisking away previous energy or blowing our breath on it.

With the shower celebrated, room prepared, all clothing washed in natural detergent, and all other gifts and toys cleansed, we were as prepared as we could possibly be for the actual birth.

During the Birth

As part of her earth-based beliefs, my daughter employed a doula to assist her through the birth experience. For those who may not know what a doula is or does, this is the simplified definition I received. A doula is trained to see to the needs of the mother exclusively during the birthing process, unlike a midwife, who is trained to see to the needs of both the mother and the baby but to concentrate more on the baby. Midwives, in addition to doctors and nurse practitioners, were part of the OB/GYN group my daughter chose; the doula was an outside contractor welcomed to the process. Midwives provide support and empowerment to the mother. In our experience, the doula brought a powerful energy with her. I was not in the birthing room (more on that later), and I was very grateful to the Lady for providing this calm and composed woman to assist my daughter. The presence, the very essence, of Gaia was unmistakable.

As stated earlier, my daughter is quite sensitive to the power and energy of crystals. She can feel and channel the magical energy in natural stones, gemstones, and minerals in a way that I find amazing. To assist in childbirth, she chose two special stones from her collection.

Bloodstone: A typical bloodstone is composed of green chalcedony flecked with red jasper. This stone promotes stamina and endurance and encourages inner strength.

Malachite: This mineral consists of hydrated copper carbonate. Known as the "midwife stone," malachite stimulates contractions, eases labor pains, and facilitates a safe childbirth.

During labor, these stones were kept by my daughter's feet, keeping her grounded with the energy flowing through her from the bottom up. I wished to place a knife under the bed to cut the pain, as my beliefs are very attuned to objects. However, my daughter vetoed that idea. This brings me to the topic of what she wanted and what I wanted, and who prevailed.

As I study and continue to learn about earth-based beliefs, the single most important part of my personal creed has become casting aside negative energy. Passing that belief along to my daughter has, to my surprise,

> **As I study and continue to learn about earth-based beliefs, the single most important part of my personal creed has become casting aside negative energy.**

created differences of opinion. The one major conflict we experienced at the birth of my granddaughter was deciding who would be in attendance. Who would be in the birthing room and who would be in the waiting room, and when? I was quite adamant that I would be in the birthing room, so it was quite a disappointment for me to learn that this would not be happening. In order to create only positive energy, I accepted this decision.

But there was one area where I held firm. My daughter expressed the wish that no one be in the waiting room of the hospital during her labor. She did not want to be concerned about or distracted by anyone or anything except the birth process. When she called to say they were on their way to the hospital, I knew I was not going to be able to abide by that directive. I lit a candle, asked for blessings (and forgiveness), and went to the hospital. Her stepmother and I waited together with love and good intentions during the time it took for our granddaughter to arrive. My daughter was mildly annoyed, but I had to do what I felt was best for my positive energy. And I can assure you my daughter spent very little time worrying about anyone in the waiting room.

After the Birth

And so we all entered into a new family configuration. From the very first, public interaction was limited to the point that only immediate family members were allowed. Modern science/medicine and ancient ways and beliefs: these two worlds live side by side and overlap in much of life. In the ongoing worldwide conversation regarding vaccines, my pagan/earth-based daughter is definitely on the side of science. No one—no grandparent, aunt, or uncle, no family member or friend—was allowed near her baby if they had not received a flu shot. I had to get a vaccine for whooping cough.

Child rearing is ruled by parental instinct. Armed with the positive attitude and intentions of everyone around her, Aurora benefited from earth-based beliefs in several ways during the first couple months of her life.

Swaddling

As a way to comfort babies and assist them in sleeping, wrapping little ones in tight but not-too-tight soft blankets has come back in style.

Bottle versus Breast

Prior to the birth, my daughter went back and forth on this issue. Her final decision was to breastfeed and to pump in order to store some of the milk. Unfortunately, even with the best of intentions and employing some gratitude spells for abundance, this did not work out and she was forced to discontinue breastfeeding. The feeding station set up in the kitchen—having been properly cleansed and blessed—now holds containers of formula (also blessed) and all that is required for homemade baby food.

Daycare

My daughter is one of those extremely fortunate people who loves her career and is very good at it. There was never a question of her returning to work, which meant finding daycare. Since she had worked at a quality nationwide childcare chain while in college, there was also no question of where Aurora would be placed. A business such as this cannot be

I add my own personal blessing from afar, wrapping the daycare in a bubble of protection. I do this with my daughter and son-in-law's home and their vehicles as well, every day.

smudged or cleansed. What can be done is, as always, to have good intentions and positive thoughts, and to cleanse and bless every item that comes with baby. Additionally, I add my own personal blessing from afar, wrapping the daycare in a bubble of protection. I do this with my daughter and son-in-law's home and their vehicles as well, every day.

Once the baby's public appearances begin, and especially after being around the other children in daycare, exposure to all the germs (good and bad) brings the first of the illnesses: the stuffy nose. The following recipe almost always brings relief and is suitable for infants who are three months and older.

ESSENTIAL OIL POTION TO COUNTER INFANT NASAL CONGESTION

- 5 drops lavender essential oil
- 5 drops lemon essential oil
- A 15 ml rollerball container
- Fractionated coconut oil

Place the drops in the rollerball container and fill with fractionated coconut oil. Shake well and apply to bottoms of feet.

TEETHING

So many options, so much advice. Old ways, new ways. New ways influenced by ancient knowledge. Amber can be used to soothe teething discomfort. When I first heard that my daughter had bought an amber for Aurora, I was appalled, thinking the baby would be chewing on the amber. All I could think of was the choking hazard. A quick internet search set me straight. I felt such relief when I realized that the amber is a necklace, not a teether. According to proponents of this way to soothe teething discomfort, Baltic amber contains a natural analgesic called succinic acid. When a baby wears the necklace, their body heat stimulates the release of this magical chemical from the gemstone, and it gets absorbed into the skin, thereby easing their pain. There is a difference of opinion as to whether the amber must be Baltic, just as there is disagreement as to whether it actually works and if it is indeed a choking hazard. As with almost all parenting advice, the information must be examined and decisions made based on that information. Personally, I prefer a drop of whiskey rubbed on the gums, but that was vetoed. Oh well.

· · · · · · · · · · · · ·

We are not the most elaborate of Wiccan families. No daily ceremonies at dawn or dusk. No swooping, sweeping capes or dresses. No skyclad romps in the light of the full moon. Nor do we have a family tradition going back generation after generation. Coming to this path later in life, I find that certain elements of other belief systems filter through and color my honor of all things earth-based. The same holds true for my daughter. Raised in a religion of saints, she has held on to the open-minded wonder and belief that a long-dead person performed miracles and continues to watch over and protect us. She is attuned to the earth. As an empath, she is powerfully attuned to others. These qualities make everyday family life mystical and create opportunities for special occasions to be celebrated with something just a little more elaborate. Something numinous. Something magical.

Emyme *has been writing for several years, and those years have brought some changes. Her daughter, one perfect Rose, has given her a granddaughter, the beloved Aurora. This places Emyme firmly and happily in crone status. One cat continues to garner all the rest of her love. Retirement looms on the horizon, which will finally provide her with more time to write. All is well. Life is good. Contact Emyme at Catsmeow24@verizon.net.*

Planning and Running Group Rituals

Deborah Castellano

Group ritual is so very full of highs and lows. When it works, it can be a genuinely life-changing experience full of meaningful insights and breakthroughs. When it doesn't work, it can feel really crummy to have put so much time into something that was spiritually meaningful to you...but apparently not to anyone else.

Whether you are putting together a main invocation for a festival or Pagan Pride Day, organizing a full moon ritual for your coven of six, or planning a Samhain rite for fifty of your closest druids, there's a lot of planning that's involved on both a spiritual and a practical level to make sure everyone gets as much as they can out of your rite.

You Can't Control It All

This is a really important starting place. Let's talk about your coven of six. Let's say you've done everything you could think of to make it a fantastic rite for all six people. You made sure to have a vegan entrée for Steve. You timed your ritual to be over by 10:00 p.m. for Aija to get home to the babysitter. You vacuumed up all the cat hair on everything for Chen. You remembered that Margo is allergic to incense. You were careful to provide a comfortable chair for Jose. You selected inclusive language especially for Pat. You picked ritual work and deities that resonate with all six people. If any one of your people had a terrible day full of calamity (a fight with their romantic partner, the boss made them stay late, new childcare had to be found, paper cuts, migraines, whatever), it doesn't matter what acts of kindness you have performed if the weather in their individual heads is not good. Sure, if your coven mates are generally stand-up people, they will appreciate the kindness shown. They will do their best to try to be present both magically and mundanely. They will try to get their heads in the game, but…we've all been there. Sometimes it's not possible. Sometimes it's monsooning in your coven mate's head despite their best efforts. But maybe everyone else's head is good and the one coven member is just happy to be there. That still makes for a really good ritual. But if everyone's brain is blizzarding, maybe you order a pizza and watch *Practical Magic* with margaritas and reschedule the ritual. That's okay too.

Let's take a bigger event. You're really not going to be able to run a ritual for fifty people who are all completely into it unless you're running a cult. It just doesn't work that way. Maybe two people had a fight in the car on the way over and they're too busy trying to beam nasty thoughts into each other's heads to be truly present, or maybe three

people aren't into that particular pantheon, or maybe seven people are too busy thinking about their feet falling asleep or how hot it is or how cold it is to give it their all. That's okay too. Your goal is to reach most people, not all people. Don't be offended if a few people wander off toward the merchants or start drinking beer on the porch. It just makes it easier for everyone else to focus.

Get Practical

You need to consider a lot of things for a group ritual to work, especially one for a larger group. If it is for ten people or more, get between one and ten people on a planning board. It can be through email, over Skype, in Martha's living room, whatever. Unless you are incredibly experienced in running group ritual, you will not think of everything. Even if you are incredibly experienced, you will inevitably not think of something. Other people can help with that, and enlisting their help ensures that they will be invested in the success of your beautiful, perfect ritual. If you can't get anyone to help, then that may be a ritual better done solo, friend, because your ideas aren't resonating with other people. Having others actively participate in the planning and running of the ritual will make your ritual come alive with many different voices and points of view, which will make it a better experience for everyone instead of a one-person band. Pick one or two things

You will inevitably not think of something. Other people can help with that, and enlisting their help ensures that they will be invested in the success of your beautiful, perfect ritual.

that you are set on (the time of day, the deities, the holiday, a song, etc.) and dig your feet in about that. Be prepared to have a very open mind and to be flexible about everything else.

Consider practical issues. If it's an outdoor ritual, have an indoor version in mind just in case. If it's a very long ritual, have seating in mind. Will you eat before or after? Will you have a kitchen witch to put the feast together? Will you have volunteers on hand to help the people who don't know the ritual format, to walk them through it and introduce them to other people? Will you have what my grove calls a "pre-ritual rap," where we assign ritual parts to others, explain the ritual layout, explain our grove's etiquette for the ritual, tell a little about the deity, run through the songs and responses, and talk about the working/invocation? People will be a lot more likely to participate if they understand what's going to happen. Bonus points if escape routes are offered, because that will make people more inclined to stay.

Spirituality Needs Planning Too

In my own experience, if you feel called to work with a new deity for a ritual, you need well over a month to get acquainted through offerings, vigils, drawing down, drawing omens, research, or however you get close to a new deity. Working with a new deity for a ritual is not something you can simply wing; the ritual will feel rote that way. Invocation should come from the heart, not from a script—unless you panic. Then you might want a backup script. Rote is better than dead air!

Do your research and do your vigils. Take time to get to know this deity. Take time to work on the magical workings. The more time you take with the spiritual aspect of the ritual, the more deeply meaningful it will be for everyone. Open yourself to your invocation and don't worry about what other people will think. Let the spirit guide you. It may not resonate with everyone, but it will be sincere. Sincerity counts both for

You are establishing a relationship with the spirit(s) you are working with. When you open yourself up like that, there's always the chance that they still may not be that into you, just like in human relationships. If that happens, you may need to revise your plans.

your fellow ritual mates and for the deities and season being celebrated. Get rooted in the moment and what's happening in your world. Make connections to the other ritual celebrants and with the spirits.

You are establishing a relationship with the spirit(s) you are working with. When you open yourself up like that, there's always the chance that they still may not be that into you, just like in human relationships. If that happens, you may need to revise your plans. You don't want spirits who don't want to be there overseeing your magical endeavors, and you don't want a reluctant guest of honor. In my experience, generally you know within a week or two if everything is gelling through omens, dreams, and trancework. If it's not, then you still have enough time to adjust if you've given yourself a couple months to prepare. Even if it's a goddess with whom you have a preexisting relationship or from whom you have received favorable prophecy in working together, there's still always the chance that they won't show up. Deities have their own agendas too. I've never had that happen when I did all of the needed prep work, however.

Remember Why You're Doing This

Sometimes, in the bustle of ritual planning, it can be easy to lose sight of what you are trying to accomplish. Very few people will ever know how much time, effort, energy, and money went into planning the ritual (which is another reason why it's good to have a planning committee, so at least they know and understand). Some may not even get the point of the ritual because they weren't there to see it shifting and evolving. If you struggle with chronic conditions, it can be difficult not to get lost under the weight of them and to stay focused on what moved you to do all this work for your deities and community. You may be stressed from planning your ritual and dealing with last-minute issues: Miriam has a head cold and can't invoke the Earth Mother, Anthony isn't coming now because Phillip will be there, Felix didn't know this was an adult-only ritual and brought little Max, or Alexa forgot to bring the roasted chicken, which was most of the feast. When you're breathing into a brown paper bag, it can be difficult to remember why you ever thought this would be a good idea. But it is something you felt called to do, and that's sacred and profound in its own right. If you can take a moment to recall why you wanted to do this in the first place and try to stay focused on that, your ritual will be much more likely to stay on track.

Details Matter

If you take enough time to plan your ritual, you'll have the chance to add little touches that will make the ritual more memorable for yourself, your ritual mates, and your spirits. Your mother may be more inclined to grant you a small favor if you show up at her house with her favorite pastry and flowers, and spirits aren't any different. Everyone appreciates effort, and it doesn't have to cost a lot. Going into debt for a ritual isn't wise, so here are some things you could do to enhance your ritual without breaking the bank:

- Craft a table runner from an old curtain for the feast table
- Get a bouquet of fresh flowers for the altar
- Get beeswax candles
- Craft tiny favors for the ritual participants
- Do henna painting if it goes with what you're trying to do
- Make a special treat for the feast
- Sew a dress to wear
- Make a doll for your deity
- Make a ritual playlist
- Get s'mores for the bonfire afterward
- Make a special incense
- Write a poem
- Go thrifting for altar gear

However you enjoy expressing yourself, try to incorporate that into your ritual, because it's one more way to make the ritual more meaningful for everyone.

Let Go

Perhaps the hardest part is letting go of the ritual as you step into it to give it space to be what it needs to be. You have put a lot of effort into this with other people who have also made a big effort, and now you're going to open the floor to people who just wandered in for the ritual. They haven't been baking the bread; they're there to eat it. And while that can sometimes be annoying, too much bread leads to having to throw away moldy bread, so you need them there too. When you involve other people, the ritual may veer in a direction that you didn't expect it to take, but your job is to gently steer the ship to stay more or less on course to accomplish your goal. But if it's going irrevocably off course, it's also your job to attempt to accept the new direction with as much grace and good cheer as possible. Forcing a ritual to stay on track doesn't put anyone in a good mood, spirits included. And you never know, that direction may give you a new experience that you never knew you wanted but are grateful to have.

Deborah Castellano's *book* Glamour Magic: The Witchcraft Revolution to Get What You Want *is available for purchase at your favorite bookstore. She writes about glamour magic at* Charmed, I'm Sure *(http://www.charmedfinishingschool.com). Her craft shop, The Mermaid & The Crow (http://www.mermaidandcrow.com), specializes in handmade goods made from 100 percent local, sustainable sources, featuring tempting small-batch ritual oils and hand-spun, hand-dyed yarn in luxe fibers and more! In a previous life, Deborah founded the first Neo-Victorian/Steampunk convention, SalonCon, which received rave reviews from con-goers and interviews from the* New York Times *and MTV. She resides in New Jersey with her husband, Jow, and their cat, Max II. She has a terrible reality television habit she can't shake and likes St. Germain liqueur, record players, and typewriters.*

Lotion Potions for Daily Self-Care and Magickal First Aid

Estha McNevin

Try as I might to stay on top of my game, there are times in the calendar year when the rush of my schedule and the gardening or catering demands of the season leave me in want of more self-care time than I'm realistically going to get. *Whenever life gets me down, Mrs. Brown, I just remember that we're all standing on a planet that is evolving and revolving within a whole astrolabe of a galaxy.* Then I reflect on the woke wisdom of adaptive magick and recall that I happen to be one of those clever *tricksy pagan monkeys* who is quite capable of manifesting my own "needs-be-met." After all, it only takes a little alchemy and a pinch of daily planetary magick to whip up a lotion that will keep that Monty Python–worthy pep in my step.

The Proof Is in the Potion

With a few quick tips and a handful of herbs, it's easy to incorporate healthful and powerful hermetic elixirs into our daily self-care routines. Changing simple habits with the days of the week to incorporate self-nurturing will help take your magick to the next level by facilitating your physical and energetic immunity from environmental contamination or undue social/psychic influence. This type of magick is used to fortify us for change by exercising the self-discipline of daily nurturing as an act of resplendent alchemy. You, too, can transform your reactions into choices when you incorporate alchemy into something as simple as lotion.

Of Faults and Alchemists

My first three lotion experiments were fraught with naiveté and inexperience. A typical fool overexcited to *experience*, I thought I could break the law of percentages when making lotions. Very quickly I was met with failure because lotions are so prone to rot when humectants, emulsifiers, and preservatives are excluded. Through moldy and separated batches, I experimented onward. Rivaling the madness and self-sacrifice of Paphnutia the Virgin, I carried on despite repeated alchemical failures. I continued to adapt, kept on tweakin' the method, and invented new formulas by researching better ingredients until finally I felt a sense of success when the outcomes satisfied my intent. Through experience, I mastered the shadow within me who, quite frankly, wanted to quit and give up with each failure. Alchemy worked me through each disappointment until I could see that I was just another step closer to the Great Work.

Days-and-Confused Planets

When we look at the corpus of Western hermetics, we have to give a fair amount of research and understanding to planetary myth and symbolism. For our ancient ancestors, this was an exact science of teaching and storytelling. Old World pagans used Roman systems like the planetary gods, and applied them even to the days of the week to conscript prayers to the many gods as well as to impart a daily sense of cosmic awe and wonder that united everyone in cultural practices throughout the city. Our esoteric concept of the constellations was formed from comforting tribal and clan stories that now typify the ancient Western experience and drive our cultural understanding of our European ancestors by retelling them through myth.

Within this system, Monday is ruled by the moon and aligned with the zodiac sign of Cancer because it is the ovum of the week, giving birth to the flow and course of events to come. Tuesday is fixed to the planet Mars and is ruled by Aries because it has long been seen as a heavy work day. Wednesday is ruled by Mercury, a god of thought and intellect, and is typified by the intuition and mental duality of Gemini. Thursday is my favorite day of the week, ruled by Jupiter, as it is both a creative and an emotional day given over to the myths of Sagittarius the archer and Pisces the fish. Friday is still date night, after all these centuries; it is ruled by Venus and is the day for love and business deals to be sealed with a stubborn, if not fair, bottom line, as suggested by Taurus and Libra. Saturday is ruled by that Old World primordial deity Saturn, willing to devour anything that disrupts his plans for eternal control; this day is often given over to the superstition of Capricorn's devilish details or to Aquarius, typified by doing one's own thing to ground down and relax. Sunday is the day to cultivate the awareness of who we are, whether that's going to temple or church or even simply mowing the lawn. Ruled by the Sun and Leo the lion, Sunday is the day of the week often given over to philosophical repose or esoteric observation of some kind.

Making Your Own Planetary Lotions

Any basic lotion is an emulsion. Think of it as a gravy that you put on your body. You take enriched water and suspend a fatty solution into it using a fruit pectin, sugar, or starch to reform a thicker consistency by cooking and then cooling the solution to a lower temperature to promote coagulation. A fatty viscous fluid will hold air when whipped and create a more stable texture. Many emulsions, like whipped cream, are stable only when they are cold, because fresh fats melt at room temperature.

Rendered or heat-treated fats have a melting point of 90–145°F and are often a key ingredient in lip balms, salves, and lotions. This is because fats have a creamy texture that protects and conditions and also absorbs easily into the skin. When solid fats are mixed with stabilizers such as melted wax or gum resin, a light and fluffy cream is produced. Clean vegetative and fruit fats are common in cosmetic and ritual lotions because they are wonderful for extending the shelf life of the final product. Coconut butter, for example, has a shelf life 1–5 years when kept cold and out of direct sunlight.

Now let's take a look at some common ingredients and components of lotions.

BUTTER OR HARD FAT BLEND

These include nut, tree, and plant-based fats that self-emulsify below 70°F.

ELIXIR

An elixir is a water-based herbal solution that is carefully prepared to impart minerals, phytonutrients, and body conditioning alongside esoteric properties.

EMOLLIENT BLEND

These are plant-based carrier oils, fluids, or gel fats.

EMULSIFIERS

These include starches, salts, volcanic minerals, animal- and plant-based polysorbate waxes, and esterified fatty acids that keep oil and water solutions stable.

EXFOLIATES

These include salt, sand, mud, pulverized grains, husks, and plant seeds that remove dead skin, activate warming oils, and regenerate the skin's elastin.

HUMECTANTS

These are plant-based hygroscopic salts and gels that can be used for deep conditioning due to their ability to absorb and retain moisture.

OILS, TINCTURES, OR EXTRACTS

These include vegetable, tree, nut, herbs, and flowers that are prized for their aroma and phytonutrients often amalgamated with mineral-rich spring waters, liquors, vegetable glycerin, or a common carrier oil like jojoba or coconut. It is wise to avoid toxic "fragrant" oils at all costs.

PRESERVATIVES

These include salts, boric acids, and citric acids, which prevent microbial bacteria growth. Germall Plus is the preservative I most favor, as it is made for cosmetics and is both organic and safe for use on animals and small children.

Recipe: Night Cream for Deep Conditioning of the Chest, Neck, and Face

Day of the Week: Monday

Planet: Moon

Zodiac: Cancer

Intent: Psychic development

Element: Water

Alchemical Phase and Substance: Dissolution, orpiment

Human Body (Gland and Region): Corneal/pineal, brain stem

Step 1

Elixir: Steep the following ingredients until the solution reduces in temperature from 140°F to 120°F (about 15 minutes). The total filtered yield of elixir needed is 1¼ cups. Use or discard any excess elixir within 24 hours.

2½ cups fresh spring water or river water, brought to 212°F

½ cup cabbage, shredded

½ cup cucumber, shredded

3 tablespoons blue lotus petals

¼ cup papaya, shredded with skin on

¼ cup willow bark powder

Step 2

Preservatives and Humectants: Mix the following preservatives and humectants into a paste, then let it rest for 3–5 minutes to activate the antimicrobial enzymes. Add this paste to the elixir when it reaches 120°F.

1 tablespoon fresh organic lime juice

1 teaspoon Liquid Germall Plus

1 teaspoon Atlantic sea salt

1 teaspoon honey powder

Step 3
Emollients: In a separate double boiler, warm the following emollient oils to 120°F over medium heat, then let rest for 15 minutes.

1 tablespoon sesame oil

2 tablespoons grapeseed oil

1 tablespoon rosehip oil

Step 4
Exfoliates: Mix the following ingredients into the elixir thoroughly until an even solution forms and all of the salt is dissolved. Keep the elixir warm at 120°F, then let rest for 5 minutes.

4 teaspoons hot springs mineral water

1 teaspoon Dead Sea clay

1 teaspoon sea salts, powdered

1 teaspoon maple sugar, powdered

2 teaspoon ground melon rind, powdered

Step 5
Butters: In a separate double boiler, warm these butters to 115°–120°F, then let sit for five minutes. Next, cover with a lid or cellophane, then place the melted butters in the fridge or on a marble slab in the kitchen. Take care to leave the thermometer in the mixture and chill it to shock

the fat until 68°F is reached. Lastly, add it to the emollient oils on the double boiler.

2 teaspoon mango butter

2 teaspoon papaya butter

Step 6
Emulsifiers: Melt wax in a separate double boil. Add the arrowroot powder to the elixir, then mix well. Next, place the beeswax in the primary double boiler bowl containing the warm emollients and butters. Maintain a temperature of 120°F.

1 teaspoon arrowroot powder

1 tablespoon beeswax

Step 7
Essential Oils: Lastly, add the following essential oils to the glass bowl along with all of the other ingredients, and remove it from the double boiler. Mix the oils in using a spatula.

2 drops tea tree essential oil

7 drops rose absolute essential oil

1 drops valerian essential oil

8 drops chamomile essential oil

2 drops lavender essential oil

Step 8

Unite all of the ingredients using an immersion blender or hand whisk. Whip the lotion for 3–5 minutes until a light and creamy consistency is achieved. Store in airtight containers while still warm, and refrigerate for 24 hours to set the lotion for best results.

Sources

Benge, Sophie. *Asian Secrets of Health, Beauty, and Relaxation.* Hong Kong: Periplus, 2000.

Faivre, Antoine. *The Eternal Hermes.* Translated by Joscelyn Godwin. Grand Rapids, MI: Phanes Press, 1995.

Roob, Alexander. *Alchemy & Mysticism: The Hermetic Museum.* New York: Taschen, 1980.

Stavish, Mark. *The Path of Alchemy.* Woodbury, MN: Llewellyn, 2006.

Stocking, Charles H., and Elmon L. Cataline. *Arithmetic of Pharmacy.* Based on the original text by Alviso B. Stevens. New York: Van Nostrand, 1952.

Whitcomb, Bill. *The Magician's Companion.* St. Paul, MN: Llewellyn, 2002.

Estha McNevin *(Missoula, MT) is a Priestess and Eastern Hellenistic oracle of Opus Aima Obscuræ, a nonprofit Matriarchal Pagan Temple Haus. Since 2003 she has dedicated her time as a ceremonialist psychic, lecturer, freelance author, and artist. In addition to hosting public sabbats, Estha organizes annual philanthropic fundraisers, teaches classes, manages the temple farm, organizes Full Moon spellcrafting ceremonies, and officiates for the women's divination rituals at each Dark Moon. To learn more, visit www.opusaimaobscurae.org and www.facebook.com/opusaimaobscurae.*

The Lunar Calendar

September 2019 to December 2020

SEPTEMBER

S	M	T	W	T	F	S
1	2	3	4	5	6	7
8	9	10	11	12	13	14
15	16	17	18	19	20	21
22	23	24	25	26	27	28
29	30					

OCTOBER

S	M	T	W	T	F	S
		1	2	3	4	5
6	7	8	9	10	11	12
13	14	15	16	17	18	19
20	21	22	23	24	25	26
27	28	29	30	31		

NOVEMBER

S	M	T	W	T	F	S
					1	2
3	4	5	6	7	8	9
10	11	12	13	14	15	16
17	18	19	20	21	22	23
24	25	26	27	28	29	30

DECEMBER

S	M	T	W	T	F	S
1	2	3	4	5	6	7
8	9	10	11	12	13	14
15	16	17	18	19	20	21
22	23	24	25	26	27	28
29	30	31				

2020

JANUARY

S	M	T	W	T	F	S
			1	2	3	4
5	6	7	8	9	10	11
12	13	14	15	16	17	18
19	20	21	22	23	24	25
26	27	28	29	30	31	

FEBRUARY

S	M	T	W	T	F	S
						1
2	3	4	5	6	7	8
9	10	11	12	13	14	15
16	17	18	19	20	21	22
23	24	25	26	27	28	29

MARCH

S	M	T	W	T	F	S
1	2	3	4	5	6	7
8	9	10	11	12	13	14
15	16	17	18	19	20	21
22	23	24	25	26	27	28
29	30	31				

APRIL

S	M	T	W	T	F	S
			1	2	3	4
5	6	7	8	9	10	11
12	13	14	15	16	17	18
19	20	21	22	23	24	25
26	27	28	29	30		

MAY

S	M	T	W	T	F	S
					1	2
3	4	5	6	7	8	9
10	11	12	13	14	15	16
17	18	19	20	21	22	23
24	25	26	27	28	29	30
31						

JUNE

S	M	T	W	T	F	S
	1	2	3	4	5	6
7	8	9	10	11	12	13
14	15	16	17	18	19	20
21	22	23	24	25	26	27
28	29	30				

JULY

S	M	T	W	T	F	S
			1	2	3	4
5	6	7	8	9	10	11
12	13	14	15	16	17	18
19	20	21	22	23	24	25
26	27	28	29	30	31	

AUGUST

S	M	T	W	T	F	S
						1
2	3	4	5	6	7	8
9	10	11	12	13	14	15
16	17	18	19	20	21	22
23	24	25	26	27	28	29
30	31					

SEPTEMBER

S	M	T	W	T	F	S
		1	2	3	4	5
6	7	8	9	10	11	12
13	14	15	16	17	18	19
20	21	22	23	24	25	26
27	28	29	30			

OCTOBER

S	M	T	W	T	F	S
				1	2	3
4	5	6	7	8	9	10
11	12	13	14	15	16	17
18	19	20	21	22	23	24
25	26	27	28	29	30	31

NOVEMBER

S	M	T	W	T	F	S
1	2	3	4	5	6	7
8	9	10	11	12	13	14
15	16	17	18	19	20	21
22	23	24	25	26	27	28
29	30					

DECEMBER

S	M	T	W	T	F	S
		1	2	3	4	5
6	7	8	9	10	11	12
13	14	15	16	17	18	19
20	21	22	23	24	25	26
27	28	29	30	31		

SEPTEMBER 2019

SU	M	T	W
1st ♎ **1**	1st ♎ **2** ☽ v/c 4:34 am ☽ → ♏ 7:35 pm *Labor Day*	1st ♏ **3**	1st ♏ **4** ☽ v/c 6:58 am ☽ → ♐ 11:08 pm
2nd ♑ **8**	2nd ♑ **9** ☽ v/c 4:30 am ☽ → ♒ 5:24 pm	2nd ♒ **10**	2nd ♒ **11** ☽ v/c 1:22 am
3rd ♈ **15**	3rd ♈ **16** ☽ v/c 12:03 pm	3rd ♈ **17** ☽ → ♉ 6:31 am	3rd ♉ **18**
4th ♊ **22** ☽ → ♋ 12:50 am	4th ♋ **23** ☉ → ♎ 3:50 am ☽ v/c 6:05 pm *Mabon* *Sun enters Libra* *Fall Equinox*	4th ♋ **24** ☽ → ♌ 5:19 am	4th ♌ **25** ☽ v/c 12:14 pm
1st ♎ **29** ☽ v/c 10:06 pm	1st ♎ **30** ☽ → ♏ 5:42 am	1	2
6	7	8	9

Eastern Daylight Time (EDT)

SEPTEMBER 2019

TH	F	SA	NOTES
1st ♐ 2nd Quarter 11:10 pm ◑	2nd ♐ 6 ☽ v/c 12:03 pm	2nd ♐ 7 ☽ → ♑ 6:37 am	
2nd ♒ 12 ☽ → ♓ 5:52 am	2nd ♓ 13	2nd ♓ ○ ☽ v/c 12:33 am Full Moon 12:33 am ☽ → ♈ 6:32 pm *Harvest Moon*	
3rd ♉ 19 ☽ v/c 9:57 am ☽ → ♊ 4:58 pm	3rd ♊ 20	3rd ♊ ◑ ☽ v/c 10:41 pm 4th Quarter 10:41 pm	
4th ♌ 26 ☽ → ♍ 6:37 am	4th ♍ 27 ☽ v/c 11:58 pm	4th ♍ ● ☽ → ♎ 6:03 am New Moon 2:26 pm *New Moon*	
3	4	5	
10	11	12	

Aspects & Moon Phases

☌ Conjunction	0°	● New Moon	(1st Quarter)
⚹ Sextile	60°	◐ Waxing Moon	(2nd Quarter)
☐ Square	90°	○ Full Moon	(3rd Quarter)
△ Trine	120°	◑ Waning Moon	(4th Quarter)
⚻ Quincunx	150°		
☍ Opposition	180°		

OCTOBER 2019

SU	M	T	W
29	**30**	1st ♏ **1**	1st ♏ ☽ v/c 5:46 am ☽ → ♐ 7:44 am **2**
2nd ♑ **6** ☽ v/c 7:25 pm ☽ → ≈ 11:42 pm	2nd ≈ **7**	2nd ≈ **8** ☽ v/c 2:27 pm	2nd ≈ **9** ☽ → ♓ 12:05 pm
2nd ♈ ○ **13** Full Moon 5:08 pm ☽ v/c 5:59 pm Blood Moon	3rd ♈ **14** ☽ → ♉ 12:24 pm	3rd ♉ **15**	3rd ♉ **16** ☽ v/c 4:37 am ☽ → ♊ 10:30 pm
3rd ♋ **20**	3rd ♋ **21** ☽ v/c 8:39 am 4th Quarter 8:39 am ☽ → ♌ 12:29 pm	4th ♌ **22**	4th ♌ **23** ☽ v/c 5:14 am ☉ → ♏ 1:20 pm ☽ → ♍ 3:29 pm Sun enters Scorpio
4th ♎ **27** ☽ v/c 4:22 am ☽ → ♏ 4:29 pm New Moon 11:39 pm New Moon	1st ♏ **28**	1st ♏ **29** ☽ v/c 1:34 pm ☽ → ♐ 5:58 pm	1st ♐ **30**
3	**4**	**5**	**6**

Eastern Daylight Time (EDT)

ZODIAC SIGNS

♈ Aries	♌ Leo	♐ Sagittarius
♉ Taurus	♍ Virgo	♑ Capricorn
♊ Gemini	♎ Libra	≈ Aquarius
♋ Cancer	♏ Scorpio	♓ Pisces

PLANETS

☉ Sun	♃ Jupiter
☽ Moon	♄ Saturn
☿ Mercury	♅ Uranus
♀ Venus	♆ Neptune
♂ Mars	♇ Pluto

OCTOBER 2019

TH	F	SA	NOTES
1st ♐ **3**	1st ♐ **4** ☽ v/c 3:34 am ☽ → ♑ 1:43 pm	1st ♑ **● 4** 2nd Quarter 12:47 pm	
2nd ♓ **10**	2nd ♓ **11** ☽ v/c 5:55 am	2nd ♓ **12** ☽ → ♈ 12:46 am	
3rd ♊ **17**	3rd ♊ **18** ☽ v/c 10:14 pm	3rd ♊ **19** ☽ → ♋ 6:43 am	
4th ♍ **24**	4th ♍ **25** ☽ v/c 9:00 am ☽ → ♎ 4:20 pm	4th ♎ **26**	
1st ♐ **31** ☽ v/c 10:30 am ☿ ℞ 11:41 am ☽ → ♑ 10:38 pm *Samhain* *Halloween* *Mercury retrograde*	**1**	**2**	
7	**8**	**9**	

ASPECTS & MOON PHASES

☌ Conjunction	0°	● New Moon	(1st Quarter)
✶ Sextile	60°	◐ Waxing Moon	(2nd Quarter)
☐ Square	90°	○ Full Moon	(3rd Quarter)
△ Trine	120°	◐ Waning Moon	(4th Quarter)
⚻ Quincunx	150°		
☍ Opposition	180°		

NOVEMBER 2019

SU	M	T	W
27	28	29	30
3 1st ♑ ☽ v/c 1:46 am ☽ → ♒ 6:19 am *Daylight Saving Time ends at 2:00 am*	**4** 1st ♒ 2nd Quarter 5:23 am ◑	**5** 2nd ♒ ☽ v/c 9:37 am ☽ → ♓ 6:08 pm *Election Day (general)*	**6** 2nd ♓
10 2nd ♈ ☽ v/c 9:00 am ☽ → ♉ 6:18 pm	**11** 2nd ♉	**12** 2nd ♉ Full Moon 8:34 am ○ ☽ v/c 10:48 am *Mourning Moon*	**13** 3rd ♉ ☽ → ♊ 3:46 am
17 3rd ♋ ☽ v/c 3:14 pm ☽ → ♌ 4:57 pm	**18** 3rd ♌	**19** 3rd ♌ ☽ v/c 4:11 pm 4th Quarter 4:11 pm ◑ ☽ → ♍ 8:54 pm	**20** 4th ♍ ☿ D 2:12 pm *Mercury direct*
24 4th ♎ ☽ → ♏ 12:58 am	**25** 4th ♏ ☽ v/c 12:30 pm	**26** 4th ♏ ☽ → ♐ 3:11 am New Moon 10:06 am ● *New Moon*	**27** 1st ♐
1	2	3	4

Eastern Daylight Time (EDT) becomes Eastern Standard Time (EST) November 3

ZODIAC SIGNS

♈ Aries	♌ Leo	♐ Sagittarius
♉ Taurus	♍ Virgo	♑ Capricorn
♊ Gemini	♎ Libra	♒ Aquarius
♋ Cancer	♏ Scorpio	♓ Pisces

PLANETS

⊙ Sun	♃ Jupiter
☽ Moon	♄ Saturn
☿ Mercury	♅ Uranus
♀ Venus	♆ Neptune
♂ Mars	♇ Pluto

NOVEMBER 2019

TH	F	SA	NOTES
31	1st ♍ 1	1st ♍ 2	
2nd ♓ ☽ v/c 8:13 pm 7	2nd ♓ ☽ → ♈ 6:49 am 8	2nd ♈ 9	
3rd ♊ 14	3rd ♊ ☽ v/c 6:40 am ☽ → ♋ 11:15 am 15	3rd ♋ 16	
4th ♍ ☽ v/c 10:31 pm ☽ → ♎ 11:20 pm 21	4th ♎ ☉ → ♐ 9:59 am 22 *Sun enters Sagittarius*	4th ♎ ☽ v/c 9:49 pm 23	
1st ♐ ☽ v/c 5:50 am ☽ → ♍ 7:33 am 28 *Thanksgiving Day*	1st ♍ ☽ v/c 10:57 pm 29	1st ♍ ☽ → ♒ 3:13 pm 30	
5	6	7	

ASPECTS & MOON PHASES

☌ Conjunction	0°	● New Moon (1st Quarter)
⚹ Sextile	60°	◑ Waxing Moon (2nd Quarter)
☐ Square	90°	○ Full Moon (3rd Quarter)
△ Trine	120°	◐ Waning Moon (4th Quarter)
⚻ Quincunx	150°	
☍ Opposition	180°	

DECEMBER 2019

SU	M	T	W
1st ≈ **1**	1st ≈ **2** ☽ v/c 7:27 am	1st ≈ **3** ☽ → ♓ 2:11 am	1st ♓ ◑ 2nd Quarter 1:58 am
2nd ♈ **8** ☽ → ♉ 2:29 am	2nd ♉ **9** ☽ v/c 8:13 pm	2nd ♉ **10** ☽ → ♊ 11:47 am	2nd ♊ **11**
3rd ♌ **15**	3rd ♌ **16** ☽ v/c 5:10 pm	3rd ♌ **17** ☽ → ♍ 2:16 am	3rd ♍ ◐ 4th Quarter 11:57 pm
4th ♏ **22** ☽ v/c 10:27 pm	4th ♏ **23** ☽ → ♐ 11:34 am	4th ♐ **24** *Christmas Eve*	4th ♐ **25** ☽ v/c 6:18 am ☽ → ♑ 4:45 pm *Christmas Day*
1st ≈ **29**	1st ≈ **30** ☽ v/c 5:24 am ☽ → ♓ 10:41 am	1st ♓ **31** *New Year's Eve*	♊ **1**
5	**6**	**7**	**8**

Eastern Standard Time (EST)

ZODIAC SIGNS

♈ Aries	♌ Leo	♐ Sagittarius
♉ Taurus	♍ Virgo	♑ Capricorn
♊ Gemini	♎ Libra	≈ Aquarius
♋ Cancer	♏ Scorpio	♓ Pisces

PLANETS

☉ Sun	♃ Jupiter
☽ Moon	♄ Saturn
☿ Mercury	♅ Uranus
♀ Venus	♆ Neptune
♂ Mars	♇ Pluto

DECEMBER 2019

TH	F	SA	NOTES
5 2nd ♓︎ ☽ v/c 3:15 am ☽ → ♈︎ 2:44 pm	**6** 2nd ♈︎	**7** 2nd ♈︎ ☽ v/c 10:01 am	
○ 12 2nd ♊︎ ☽ v/c 12:12 am Full Moon 12:12 am ☽ → ♋︎ 6:23 pm *Long Nights Moon*	**13** 3rd ♋︎	**14** 3rd ♋︎ ☽ v/c 10:57 am ☽ → ♌︎ 10:56 am	
19 4th ♍︎ ☽ v/c 3:07 am ☽ → ♎︎ 5:04 am	**20** 4th ♎︎	**21** 4th ♎︎ ☽ v/c 6:45 am ☽ → ♏︎ 7:57 am ☉ → ♑︎ 11:19 pm *Yule* *Sun enters Capricorn* *Winter Solstice*	
● 26 4th ♑︎ New Moon 12:13 am *New Moon* *Solar Eclipse*	**27** 1st ♑︎ ☽ v/c 4:03 pm	**28** 1st ♑︎ ☽ → ♒︎ 12:21 am	
2	**3**	**4**	
9	**10**	**11**	

JANUARY 2020

SU	M	T	W
29	30	31	1 1st ♓ ☽ v/c 9:14 pm ☽ → ♈ 11:00 pm *New Year's Day*
5 2nd ♉	6 2nd ♉ ☽ v/c 7:08 am ☽ → ♊ 9:11 pm	7 2nd ♊	8 2nd ♊ ☽ v/c 5:16 pm
12 3rd ♌	13 3rd ♌ ☽ v/c 8:42 am ☽ → ♍ 9:06 am ♀ → ♓ 1:39 pm	14 3rd ♍	15 3rd ♍ ☽ v/c 7:12 am ☽ → ♎ 10:43 am
19 4th ♏ ☽ v/c 4:22 pm ☽ → ♐ 5:41 pm	20 4th ♐ ☉ → ♒ 9:55 am ☽ v/c 11:46 pm *Sun enters Aquarius* *Martin Luther King Jr. Day*	21 4th ♐	22 4th ♑ ☽ → ♑ 12:00 am
26 1st ♒ ☽ → ♓ 6:44 pm	27 1st ♓	28 1st ♓ ☽ v/c 8:08 pm	29 1st ♓ ☽ → ♈ 6:51 am
2	3	4	5

Eastern Standard Time (EST)

ZODIAC SIGNS

♈ Aries	♌ Leo	♐ Sagittarius
♉ Taurus	♍ Virgo	♑ Capricorn
♊ Gemini	♎ Libra	♒ Aquarius
♋ Cancer	♏ Scorpio	♓ Pisces

PLANETS

☉ Sun	♃ Jupiter
☽ Moon	♄ Saturn
☿ Mercury	♅ Uranus
♀ Venus	♆ Neptune
♂ Mars	♇ Pluto

JANUARY 2020

TH	F	SA	NOTES
1st ♈ 2nd Quarter 11:45 pm ◑	2nd ♈ 3 ♂ → ♐ 4:37 am ☽ v/c 8:18 pm	2nd ♈ 4 ☽ → ♉ 11:15 am	
2nd ♊ 9 ☽ → ♋ 3:43 am	2nd ♋ ◯ Full Moon 2:21 pm ☽ v/c 6:58 pm ♅ D 8:49 pm *Cold Moon* *Lunar Eclipse*	3rd ♋ 11 ☽ → ♌ 7:16 am	
3rd ♎ 16 ☿ → ♒ 1:31 pm	3rd ♎ ◑ ☽ v/c 7:58 am 4th Quarter 7:58 am ☽ → ♏ 1:20 pm	4th ♏ 18	
4th ♑ 23 ☽ v/c 9:08 pm	4th ♑ ● ☽ → ♒ 8:20 am New Moon 4:42 pm *New Moon*	1st ♒ 25 ☽ v/c 2:06 pm	
1st ♈ 30	1st ♈ 31 ☽ v/c 10:10 am ☽ → ♉ 7:28 pm	1	
6	7	8	

FEBRUARY 2020

SU	M	T	W
26	27	28	29
2 2nd ♉ Imbolc Groundhog Day	**3** 2nd ♉ ☽ v/c 6:28 am ☽ → ♊ 6:29 am ☿ → ♓ 6:37 am	**4** 2nd ♊	**5** 2nd ♊ ☽ v/c 9:20 am ☽ → ♋ 2:03 pm
9 2nd ♌ Full Moon 2:33 am ☽ v/c 11:08 am ☽ → ♍ 6:39 pm Quickening Moon	**10** 3rd ♍	**11** 3rd ♍ ☽ v/c 1:26 pm ☽ → ♎ 6:37 pm	**12** 3rd ♎ s
16 4th ♐ ♂ → ♑ 6:33 am ☿ ℞ 7:54 pm Mercury retrograde	**17** 4th ♐ Presidents' Day	**18** 4th ♐ ☽ v/c 4:03 am ☽ → ♑ 5:37 am ☉ → ♓ 11:57 pm Sun enters Pisces	**19** 4th ♑
23 4th ♒ ☽ → ♓ 1:37 am New Moon 10:32 am New Moon	**24** 1st ♓	**25** 1st ♓ ☽ v/c 9:12 am ☽ → ♈ 1:47 pm	**26** 1st ♈
1	2	3	4

Eastern Standard Time (EST)

Zodiac Signs

♈ Aries	♌ Leo	♐ Sagittarius
♉ Taurus	♍ Virgo	♑ Capricorn
♊ Gemini	♎ Libra	♒ Aquarius
♋ Cancer	♏ Scorpio	♓ Pisces

Planets

☉ Sun	♃ Jupiter
☽ Moon	♄ Saturn
☿ Mercury	♅ Uranus
♀ Venus	♆ Neptune
♂ Mars	♇ Pluto

FEBRUARY 2020

TH	F	SA	NOTES
30	31	1st ♉ 2nd Quarter 8:42 pm ◐	
2nd ♋ 6	2nd ♋ 7 ☽ v/c 10:43 am ♀ → ♈ 3:02 pm ☽ → ♌ 5:45 pm	2nd ♌ 8	
3rd ♎ 13 ☽ v/c 4:40 pm ☽ → ♏ 7:37 pm	3rd ♏ 14 Valentine's Day	3rd ♏ 15 ◑ 4th Quarter 5:17 pm ☽ v/c 5:20 pm ☽ → ♐ 11:07 pm	
4th ♑ 20 ☽ v/c 9:18 am ☽ → ♒ 2:42 pm	4th ♒ 21 ☽ v/c 11:08 pm	4th ♒ 22	
1st ♈ 27 ☽ v/c 10:25 pm	1st ♈ 28 ☽ → ♉ 2:30 am	1st ♉ 29	
5	6	7	

ASPECTS & MOON PHASES

☌ Conjunction	0°	● New Moon (1st Quarter)
✶ Sextile	60°	◑ Waxing Moon (2nd Quarter)
☐ Square	90°	○ Full Moon (3rd Quarter)
△ Trine	120°	◐ Waning Moon (4th Quarter)
⚻ Quincunx	150°	
☍ Opposition	180°	

MARCH 2020

SU	M	T	W
1 1st ♉ ☽ v/c 10:52 am ☽ → ♊ 2:21 pm	**2** 1st ♊ 2nd Quarter 2:57 pm ◑	**3** 2nd ♊ ☽ v/c 9:20 pm ☽ → ♋ 11:25 pm	**4** 2nd ♋ ☿ → ♒ 6:08 am ♀ → ♉ 10:07 pm
8 2nd ♌ ☽ v/c 4:12 am ☽ → ♍ 6:47 am *Daylight Saving Time begins at 2:00 am*	**9** 2nd ♍ Full Moon 1:48 pm ○ ☿ D 11:49 pm *Storm Moon Mercury direct*	**10** 3rd ♍ ☽ v/c 4:32 am ☽ → ♎ 6:03 am	**11** 3rd ♎
15 3rd ♐	**16** 3rd ♐ ☿ → ♓ 3:42 am ☽ v/c 5:34 am 4th Quarter 5:34 am ◐ ☽ → ♑ 12:25 pm	**17** 4th ♑ *St. Patrick's Day*	**18** 4th ♑ ☽ v/c 8:48 pm ☽ → ♒ 9:16 pm
22 4th ♓	**23** 4th ♓ ☽ v/c 10:51 am ☽ → ♈ 8:58 pm	**24** 4th ♈ New Moon 5:28 am ● *New Moon*	**25** 1st ♈
29 1st ♊	**30** 1st ♊ ☽ v/c 11:10 am ♂ → ♒ 3:43 pm	**31** 1st ♊ ☽ → ♋ 7:43 am	**1**
5	**6**	**7**	**8**

Eastern Standard Time (EST) becomes Eastern Daylight Time (EDT) March 8

ZODIAC SIGNS

♈ Aries	♌ Leo	♐ Sagittarius
♉ Taurus	♍ Virgo	♑ Capricorn
♊ Gemini	♎ Libra	♒ Aquarius
♋ Cancer	♏ Scorpio	♓ Pisces

PLANETS

☉ Sun	♃ Jupiter
☽ Moon	♄ Saturn
☿ Mercury	♅ Uranus
♀ Venus	♆ Neptune
♂ Mars	♇ Pluto

MARCH 2020

TH	F	SA	NOTES
5 2nd ⊗	**6** 2nd ⊗ ☽ v/c 2:11 am ☽ → ♌ 4:27 am	**7** 2nd ♌	
12 3rd ♎ ☽ v/c 4:12 am ☽ → ♏ 5:28 am	**13** 3rd ♏	**14** 3rd ♏ ☽ v/c 6:06 am ☽ → ♐ 7:09 am	
19 4th ♒ ☉ → ♈ 11:50 pm *Ostara* *Sun enters Aries* *Spring Equinox*	**20** 4th ♒ ☽ v/c 5:00 am	**21** 4th ♒ ☽ → ♓ 8:33 am ♄ → ♒ 11:58 pm	
26 1st ♈ ☽ v/c 3:16 am ☽ → ♉ 9:37 am	**27** 1st ♉	**28** 1st ♉ ☽ v/c 7:05 pm ☽ → ♊ 9:38 pm	
2	**3**	**4**	
9	**10**	**11**	

Aspects & Moon Phases

☌ Conjunction	0°	● New Moon	(1st Quarter)
✶ Sextile	60°	◐ Waxing Moon	(2nd Quarter)
□ Square	90°	○ Full Moon	(3rd Quarter)
△ Trine	120°	◑ Waning Moon	(4th Quarter)
⊼ Quincunx	150°		
☍ Opposition	180°		

APRIL 2020

SU	M	T	W
29	30	31	1st ⊗ 2nd Quarter 6:21 am ◐ *All Fools' Day*
2nd ♍ 5	2nd ♍ 6 ☽ v/c 9:29 am ☽ → ♎ 5:16 pm	2nd ♎ Full Moon 10:35 pm ○ *Wind Moon*	3rd ♎ 8 ☽ v/c 8:50 am ☽ → ♏ 4:17 pm
3rd ♐ 12 ☽ v/c 7:46 am ☽ → ♑ 8:05 pm	3rd ♑ 13	3rd ♑ 4th Quarter 6:56 pm ◑	4th ♑ 15 ☽ → ♒ 3:37 am
4th ♓ 19 ☉ → ♉ 10:45 am ☽ v/c 7:31 pm *Sun enters Taurus*	4th ♓ 20 ☽ → ♈ 3:00 am	4th ♈ 21	4th ♈ ● ☽ v/c 8:32 am ☽ → ♉ 3:36 pm New Moon 10:26 pm *New Moon* *Earth Day*
1st ♊ 26	1st ♊ 27 ☽ v/c 1:00 pm ☽ → ⊗ 1:28 pm ☿ → ♉ 3:53 pm	1st ⊗ 28	1st ⊗ 29 ☽ v/c 3:29 pm ☽ → ♌ 9:06 pm
3	4	5	6

Eastern Daylight Time (EDT)

ZODIAC SIGNS

♈ Aries	♌ Leo	♐ Sagittarius
♉ Taurus	♍ Virgo	♑ Capricorn
♊ Gemini	♎ Libra	♒ Aquarius
♋ Cancer	♏ Scorpio	♓ Pisces

PLANETS

☉ Sun	♃ Jupiter
☽ Moon	♄ Saturn
☿ Mercury	♅ Uranus
♀ Venus	♆ Neptune
♂ Mars	♇ Pluto

TH	F	SA	NOTES
2 2nd ⊗ ☽ v/c 12:49 pm ☽ → ♌ 2:26 pm	**3** 2nd ♌ ♀ → ♊ 1:11 pm ☽ v/c 3:29 pm	**4** 2nd ♌ ☽ → ♍ 5:18 pm	
9 3rd ♏	**10** 3rd ♏ ☽ v/c 3:35 pm ☽ → ♐ 4:35 pm	**11** 3rd ♐ ☿ → ♈ 12:48 am	
16 4th ♒	**17** 4th ♒ ☽ v/c 10:34 am ☽ → ♓ 2:29 pm	**18** 4th ♓	
23 1st ♉	**24** 1st ♉ ☽ v/c 8:43 pm	**25** 1st ♉ ☽ → ♊ 3:20 am ♀ Rx 2:54 pm	
● 1st ♌ 2nd Quarter 4:38 pm	1	2	
7	8	9	

ASPECTS & MOON PHASES

♂ Conjunction	0°	● New Moon	(1st Quarter)
✳ Sextile	60°	◑ Waxing Moon	(2nd Quarter)
☐ Square	90°	○ Full Moon	(3rd Quarter)
△ Trine	120°	◐ Waning Moon	(4th Quarter)
⚻ Quincunx	150°		
☍ Opposition	180°		

MAY 2020

SU	M	T	W
26	27	28	29 Beltane
3 2nd ♍ ☽ v/c 10:25 pm	4 2nd ♍ ☽ → ♎ 3:09 am	5 2nd ♎ ☽ v/c 10:31 pm	6 2nd ♎ ☽ → ♏ 3:05 am
10 3rd ♐ ☽ v/c 2:11 am ☽ → ♑ 5:39 am Mother's Day	11 3rd ♑ ♄ ℞ 12:09 am ☿ → ♊ 5:58 pm	12 3rd ♑ ☽ v/c 6:30 am ☽ → ♒ 11:39 am	13 3rd ♒ ♂ → ♓ 12:17 am ♀ ℞ 2:45 am Venus retrograde
17 4th ♓ ☽ v/c 3:59 am ☽ → ♈ 9:36 am	18 4th ♈	19 4th ♈ ☽ v/c 4:33 pm ☽ → ♉ 10:10 pm	20 4th ♉ ☉ → ♊ 9:49 am Sun enters Gemini
24 1st ♊ ☽ v/c 7:09 am ☽ → ♋ 7:09 pm	25 1st ♋ Memorial Day	26 1st ♋ ☽ v/c 9:06 pm	27 1st ♋ ☽ → ♌ 2:33 am
31 2nd ♍ ☽ v/c 5:17 am ☽ → ♎ 10:38 am	1	2	3

Eastern Daylight Time (EDT)

MAY 2020

TH	F	SA	NOTES
30	1 2nd ♌︎ ☽ v/c 12:04 pm	2 2nd ♌︎ ☽ → ♍︎ 1:35 am	
2nd ♏︎ ○ Full Moon 6:45 am ☽ v/c 10:39 pm _Flower Moon_	8 3rd ♏︎ ☽ → ♐︎ 3:15 am	9 3rd ♐︎	
3rd ♒︎ ◐ ☽ v/c 10:03 am 4th Quarter 10:03 am ♃ ℞ 10:32 am ☽ → ♓︎ 9:24 pm	15 4th ♓︎	16 4th ♓︎	
4th ♉︎ 21	4th ♉︎ ● ☽ v/c 4:01 am ☽ → ♊︎ 9:36 am New Moon 1:39 pm _New Moon_	23 1st ♊︎	
1st ♌︎ 28 ☽ v/c 9:30 am ☿ → ♋︎ 2:09 pm	1st ♌︎ ◑ ☽ → ♍︎ 7:40 am 2nd Quarter 11:30 pm	30 2nd ♍︎	
4	5	6	

ASPECTS & MOON PHASES

☌ Conjunction	0°	● New Moon (1st Quarter)
⚹ Sextile	60°	◐ Waxing Moon (2nd Quarter)
☐ Square	90°	○ Full Moon (3rd Quarter)
△ Trine	120°	◑ Waning Moon (4th Quarter)
⚻ Quincunx	150°	
☍ Opposition	180°	

JUNE 2020

SU	M	T	W
31	1 2nd ♎︎	2 2nd ♎︎ ☽ v/c 6:40 am ☽ → ♏︎ 12:06 pm	3 2nd ♏︎
7 3rd ♑︎	8 3rd ♑︎ ☽ v/c 2:06 pm ☽ → ♒︎ 8:54 pm	9 3rd ♒︎	10 3rd ♒︎ ☽ v/c 10:35 am
14 4th ♈︎	15 4th ♈︎ ☽ v/c 8:49 pm	16 4th ♈︎ ☽ → ♉︎ 5:35 am	17 4th ♉︎
21 4th ♊︎ ☽ → ♋︎ 2:02 am New Moon 2:41 am *New Moon* *Solar Eclipse* *Father's Day*	22 1st ♋︎	23 1st ♋︎ ♆ ℞ 12:31 am ☽ v/c 3:20 am ☽ → ♌︎ 8:33 am	24 1st ♌︎ ☽ v/c 1:34 am
28 1st ♎︎ 2nd Quarter 4:16 am	29 2nd ♎︎ ☽ v/c 9:02 am ☽ → ♏︎ 6:48 pm	30 2nd ♏︎	1
5	6	7	8

Eastern Daylight Time (EDT)

ZODIAC SIGNS

♈︎ Aries	♌︎ Leo	♐︎ Sagittarius
♉︎ Taurus	♍︎ Virgo	♑︎ Capricorn
♊︎ Gemini	♎︎ Libra	♒︎ Aquarius
♋︎ Cancer	♏︎ Scorpio	♓︎ Pisces

PLANETS

☉ Sun	♃ Jupiter
☽ Moon	♄ Saturn
☿ Mercury	♅ Uranus
♀ Venus	♆ Neptune
♂ Mars	♇ Pluto

TH	F	SA	NOTES
4 2nd ♏ ☽ v/c 7:36 am ☽ → ♐ 1:17 pm	**○** 2nd ♐ Full Moon 3:12 pm	**6** 3rd ♐ ☽ v/c 12:10 am ☽ → ♑ 3:44 pm	
	Strong Sun Moon *Lunar Eclipse*		
11 3rd ♒ ☽ → ♓ 5:32 am	**12** 3rd ♓	**◑** 3rd ♓ 4th Quarter 2:24 am ☽ v/c 8:45 am ☽ → ♈ 5:03 pm	
18 4th ♉ ☿ ℞ 12:59 am ☽ v/c 8:02 am ☽ → ♊ 5:00 pm *Mercury retrograde*	**19** 4th ♊	**20** 4th ♊ ☉ → ♋ 5:44 pm ☽ v/c 5:48 pm *Litha* *Sun enters Cancer* *Summer Solstice*	
25 1st ♌ ♀ D 2:48 am ☽ → ♍ 1:05 pm *Venus direct*	**26** 1st ♍	**27** 1st ♍ ☽ v/c 4:02 pm ☽ → ♎ 4:16 pm ♂ → ♈ 9:45 pm	
2	3	4	
9	10	11	

Aspects & Moon Phases

☌ Conjunction	0°	● New Moon	(1st Quarter)
✶ Sextile	60°	◐ Waxing Moon	(2nd Quarter)
☐ Square	90°	○ Full Moon	(3rd Quarter)
△ Trine	120°	◑ Waning Moon	(4th Quarter)
⚻ Quincunx	150°		
☍ Opposition	180°		

JULY 2020

SU	M	T	W
28	29	30	**1** 2nd ♏ ♄ → ♐ 7:37 pm ☽ v/c 9:20 pm ☽ → ♐ 9:21 pm
5 2nd ♐ Full Moon 12:44 am ○ Blessing Moon Lunar Eclipse	**6** 3rd ♐ ☽ v/c 5:35 am ☽ → ≈ 6:08 am	**7** 3rd ≈ ☽ v/c 12:37 am	**8** 3rd ≈ ☽ → ♓ 2:13 pm
12 3rd ♈ ◐ ☿ D 4:26 am 4th Quarter 7:29 pm Mercury direct	**13** 4th ♈ ☽ v/c 11:54 am ☽ → ♉ 1:34 pm	**14** 4th ♉	**15** 4th ♉ ☽ v/c 11:21 pm
19 4th ♋	**20** 4th ♋ ● New Moon 1:33 pm ☽ v/c 1:55 pm ☽ → ♌ 4:16 pm New Moon	**21** 1st ♌ ☽ v/c 8:27 pm	**22** 1st ♌ ☉ → ♌ 4:37 am ☽ → ♍ 7:40 pm Sun enters Leo
26 1st ♎ ☽ v/c 9:09 pm	**27** 1st ♎ ◑ ☽ → ♏ 12:12 am 2nd Quarter 8:33 am	**28** 2nd ♏	**29** 2nd ♏ ☽ v/c 12:01 am ☽ → ♐ 3:25 am
2	3	4	5

Eastern Daylight Time (EDT)

ZODIAC SIGNS

♈ Aries	♌ Leo	♐ Sagittarius
♉ Taurus	♍ Virgo	♑ Capricorn
♊ Gemini	♎ Libra	≈ Aquarius
♋ Cancer	♏ Scorpio	♓ Pisces

PLANETS

☉ Sun	♃ Jupiter
☽ Moon	♄ Saturn
☿ Mercury	♅ Uranus
♀ Venus	♆ Neptune
♂ Mars	♇ Pluto

JULY 2020

TH	F	SA	NOTES
2nd ♐ 1	2nd ♐ 3 ☽ v/c 9:06 am	2nd ♐ 4 ☽ → ♑ 12:48 am *Independence Day*	
3rd ♓ 9	3rd ♓ 10 ☽ v/c 11:49 pm	3rd ♓ 11 ☽ → ♈ 1:06 am	
4th ♉ 16 ☽ → ♊ 1:19 am	4th ♊ 17 ☽ v/c 5:14 pm	4th ♊ 18 ☽ → ♋ 10:24 am	
1st ♍ 23	1st ♍ 24 ☽ v/c 7:08 pm ☽ → ♎ 9:54 pm	1st ♎ 25	
2nd ♐ 30 ☽ v/c 8:08 pm	2nd ♐ 31 ☽ → ♑ 7:58 am	1	
6	7	8	

Aspects & Moon Phases

☌ Conjunction 0°		● New Moon	(1st Quarter)
⚹ Sextile 60°		◐ Waxing Moon	(2nd Quarter)
□ Square 90°		○ Full Moon	(3rd Quarter)
△ Trine 120°		◑ Waning Moon	(4th Quarter)
⊼ Quincunx 150°			
☍ Opposition 180°			

AUGUST 2020

SU	M	T	W
26	27	28	29
2 2nd ♑ ☽ v/c 9:59 am ☽ → ≈ 2:11 pm	**3** 2nd ≈ Full Moon 11:59 am ○ *Corn Moon*	**4** 3rd ≈ ☽ v/c 5:45 pm ☽ → ♓ 10:28 pm ☿ → ♌ 11:32 pm	**5** 3rd ♓
9 3rd ♈ ☽ v/c 3:50 pm ☽ → ♉ 9:28 pm	**10** 3rd ♉	**11** 3rd ♉ 4th Quarter 12:45 pm ◑	**12** 4th ♉ ☽ v/c 3:55 am ☽ → ♊ 9:46 am
16 4th ♋ ☽ v/c 7:59 pm	**17** 4th ♋ ☽ → ♌ 1:38 am	**18** 4th ♌ New Moon 10:42 pm ● *New Moon*	**19** 1st ♌ ☽ v/c 1:38 am ☽ → ♍ 4:20 am ☿ → ♍ 9:30 pm
23 1st ♎ ☽ v/c 12:20 am ☽ → ♏ 6:16 am	**24** 1st ♏	**25** 1st ♏ ☽ v/c 2:27 am ☽ → ♐ 8:49 am 2nd Quarter 1:58 pm ◐	**26** 2nd ♐
30 2nd ≈	**31** 2nd ≈	1	2

Eastern Daylight Time (EDT)

ZODIAC SIGNS

♈ Aries	♌ Leo	♐ Sagittarius
♉ Taurus	♍ Virgo	♑ Capricorn
♊ Gemini	♎ Libra	≈ Aquarius
♋ Cancer	♏ Scorpio	♓ Pisces

PLANETS

☉ Sun	♃ Jupiter
☽ Moon	♄ Saturn
☿ Mercury	♅ Uranus
♀ Venus	♆ Neptune
♂ Mars	♇ Pluto

AUGUST 2020

TH	F	SA	NOTES
30	31	2nd ♑ 1	
Lammas			
3rd ♓ 6	3rd ♓ 7 ☽ v/c 8:53 am ☽ → ♈ 9:05 am ♀ → ♋ 11:21 am	3rd ♈ 8	
4th ♊ 13	4th ♊ 14 ☽ v/c 7:19 am ☽ → ♋ 7:35 am	4th ♋ 15 ♅ ℞ 10:25 am	
1st ♍ 20 ☽ v/c 11:37 pm	1st ♍ 21 ☽ → ♎ 5:16 am	1st ♎ 22 ☉ → ♍ 11:45 am ☽ v/c 9:20 pm *Sun enters Virgo*	
2nd ♐ 27 ☽ v/c 8:00 am ☽ → ♑ 1:37 pm	2nd ♑ 28	2nd ♑ 29 ☽ v/c 3:31 pm ☽ → ♒ 8:37 pm	
3	4	5	

ASPECTS & MOON PHASES

☌ Conjunction	0°	● New Moon	(1st Quarter)
✶ Sextile	60°	◐ Waxing Moon	(2nd Quarter)
□ Square	90°	○ Full Moon	(3rd Quarter)
△ Trine	120°	◑ Waning Moon	(4th Quarter)
⚻ Quincunx	150°		
☍ Opposition	180°		

SEPTEMBER 2020

SU	M	T	W
30	31	1 2nd ≈ ☽ v/c 12:56 am ☽ → ♓ 5:34 am	2 2nd ♓ Full Moon 1:22 am ○ *Harvest Moon*
6 3rd ♈ ☽ v/c 12:45 am ♀ → ♌ 3:22 am ☽ → ♉ 4:43 am	7 3rd ♉ *Labor Day*	8 3rd ♉ ☽ v/c 8:47 am ☽ → ♊ 5:28 pm	9 3rd ♊ ♂ ℞ 6:22 pm *Mars retrograde*
13 4th ♋ ☽ v/c 8:05 am ☽ → ♌ 11:32 am	14 4th ♌	15 4th ♌ ☽ v/c 11:09 am ☽ → ♍ 2:37 pm	16 4th ♍
20 1st ♏	21 1st ♏ ☽ v/c 2:13 pm ☽ → ♐ 3:32 pm	22 1st ♐ ☉ → ♎ 9:31 am *Mabon* *Sun enters Libra* *Fall Equinox*	22 1st ♐ ☽ v/c 1:31 pm ☽ → ♑ 7:16 pm 2nd Quarter 9:55 pm ◐
27 2nd ≈ ☿ → ♏ 3:41 am	28 2nd ≈ ☽ v/c 3:18 am ☽ → ♓ 11:34 am	29 2nd ♓ ♄ D 1:11 am	30 2nd ♓ ☽ v/c 1:30 pm ☽ → ♈ 10:47 pm
4	5	6	7

Eastern Daylight Time (EDT)

ZODIAC SIGNS

♈ Aries   ♌ Leo   ♐ Sagittarius
♉ Taurus   ♍ Virgo   ♑ Capricorn
♊ Gemini   ♎ Libra   ≈ Aquarius
♋ Cancer   ♏ Scorpio   ♓ Pisces

PLANETS

☉ Sun   ♃ Jupiter
☽ Moon   ♄ Saturn
☿ Mercury   ♅ Uranus
♀ Venus   ♆ Neptune
♂ Mars   ♇ Pluto

SEPTEMBER 2020

TH	F	SA	NOTES
3 3rd ♓︎ ☽ v/c 10:34 am ☽ → ♈︎ 4:22 pm	**4** 3rd ♈︎	**5** ☿ → ♎︎ 3:46 pm	
10 3rd ♊︎ 4th Quarter 5:26 am ◑	**11** 4th ♊︎ ☽ v/c 12:48 am ☽ → ♋︎ 4:23 am	**12** 4th ♋︎ ♃ D 8:41 pm	
17 4th ♍︎ New Moon 7:00 am ● ☽ v/c 7:42 am ☽ → ♎︎ 2:56 pm *New Moon*	**18** 1st ♎︎	**19** 1st ♎︎ ☽ v/c 10:29 am ☽ → ♏︎ 2:33 pm	
24 2nd ♑︎	**25** 2nd ♑︎ ☽ v/c 11:36 pm	**26** 2nd ♑︎ ☽ → ♒︎ 2:08 am	
1	*2*	*3*	
8	*9*	*10*	

ASPECTS & MOON PHASES

☌ Conjunction	0°	● New Moon	(1st Quarter)
✶ Sextile	60°	◐ Waxing Moon	(2nd Quarter)
□ Square	90°	○ Full Moon	(3rd Quarter)
△ Trine	120°	◑ Waning Moon	(4th Quarter)
⚻ Quincunx	150°		
☍ Opposition	180°		

OCTOBER 2020

SU	M	T	W
27	28	29	30
4 3rd ♉ ♀ D 9:32 am	**5** 3rd ♉ ☽ v/c 2:41 pm	**6** 3rd ♉ ☽ → ♊ 12:03 am	**7** 3rd ♊ ☽ v/c 9:57 pm
11 4th ♌	**12** 4th ♌ ☽ v/c 10:29 am	**13** 4th ♌ ☽ → ♍ 12:56 am ☿ ℞ 9:05 am *Mercury retrograde*	**14** 4th ♍ ☽ v/c 6:47 pm
18 1st ♏ ☽ v/c 5:43 pm	**19** 1st ♏ ☽ → ♐ 12:43 am	**20** 1st ♐ ☽ v/c 11:38 pm	**21** 1st ♐ ☽ → ♑ 2:44 am
25 2nd ♒ ☽ → ♓ 5:18 pm	**26** 2nd ♓	**27** 2nd ♓ ☽ v/c 8:46 pm ☿ → ♎ 9:33 pm ♀ → ♎ 9:41 pm	**28** 2nd ♓ ☽ → ♈ 4:45 am
1	2	3	4

Eastern Daylight Time (EDT)

ZODIAC SIGNS

♈ Aries	♌ Leo	♐ Sagittarius
♉ Taurus	♍ Virgo	♑ Capricorn
♊ Gemini	♎ Libra	♒ Aquarius
♋ Cancer	♏ Scorpio	♓ Pisces

PLANETS

☉ Sun	♃ Jupiter
☽ Moon	♄ Saturn
☿ Mercury	♅ Uranus
♀ Venus	♆ Neptune
♂ Mars	♇ Pluto

OCTOBER 2020

TH	F	SA	NOTES
1 ○ 2nd ♈ Full Moon 5:05 pm *Blood Moon*	2 3rd ♈ ♀ → ♍ 4:48 pm	3 3rd ♈ ☽ v/c 1:47 am ☽ → ♉ 11:12 am	
8 3rd ♊ ☽ → ♋ 11:45 am	9 ◑ 3rd ♋ 4th Quarter 8:40 pm	10 4th ♋ ☽ v/c 12:04 pm ☽ → ♌ 8:24 pm	
15 4th ♍ ☽ → ♎ 1:54 am	16 ● 4th ♎ New Moon 3:31 pm ☽ v/c 6:11 pm *New Moon*	17 1st ♎ ☽ → ♏ 1:05 am	
22 1st ♑ ☉ → ♏ 7:00 pm *Sun enters Scorpio*	23 ◑ 1st ♑ ☽ v/c 12:35 am ☽ → ♒ 8:17 am 2nd Quarter 9:23 am	24 2nd ♒ ☽ v/c 5:54 pm	
29 2nd ♈	30 2nd ♈ ☽ v/c 12:12 pm ☽ → ♉ 5:19 pm	31 ○ 2nd ♉ Full Moon 10:49 am *Samhain* *Halloween*	
5	6	7	

NOVEMBER 2020

SU	M	T	W
1 3rd ♉ ☽ v/c 9:29 pm *Daylight Saving Time* *ends at 2:00 am*	**2** 3rd ♉ ☽ → ♊ 5:00 am	**3** 3rd ♊ ☿ D 12:50 pm *Mercury direct* *Election Day (general)*	**4** 3rd ♊ ☽ v/c 8:49 am ☽ → ♋ 4:45 pm
8 3rd ♌ 4th Quarter 8:46 am ◐	**9** 4th ♌ ☽ v/c 6:05 am ☽ → ♍ 8:30 am	**10** 4th ♍ ☿ → ♏ 4:55 pm	**11** 4th ♍ ☽ v/c 5:58 am ☽ → ♎ 11:09 am
15 4th ♏ New Moon 12:07 am ● ☽ v/c 6:13 am ☽ → ♐ 10:47 am *New Moon*	**16** 1st ♐	**17** 1st ♐ ☽ v/c 2:55 am ☽ → ♑ 11:35 am	**18** 1st ♑
22 2nd ♓	**23** 2nd ♓	**24** 2nd ♓ ☽ v/c 5:44 am ☽ → ♈ 10:05 am	**25** 2nd ♈
29 2nd ♉ ☽ v/c 7:48 am ☽ → ♊ 11:16 am	**30** 2nd ♊ Full Moon 4:30 am ○ ☽ v/c 11:22 pm *Mourning Moon* *Lunar Eclipse*	**1**	**2**
6	**7**	**8**	**9**

Eastern Daylight Time (EDT) becomes Eastern Standard Time (EST) November 1

NOVEMBER 2020

TH	F	SA	NOTES
3rd ⊗ **5**	3rd ⊗ **6** ☽ v/c 8:27 pm	3rd ⊗ **7** ☽ → ♌ 2:18 am	
4th ♎ **12**	4th ♎ **13** ☽ v/c 6:32 am ☽ → ♏ 11:19 am ♂ D 7:36 pm *Mars direct*	4th ♏ **14**	
1st ♑ **19** ☽ v/c 11:30 am ☽ → ♒ 3:25 pm	1st ♒ **20** ☽ v/c 7:49 pm	1st ♒ **21** ◑ ♀ → ♏ 8:22 am ☉ → ♐ 3:40 pm ☽ → ♓ 11:06 pm 2nd Quarter 11:45 pm *Sun enters Sagittarius*	
2nd ♈ **26** ☽ v/c 6:46 pm ☽ → ♉ 10:43 pm *Thanksgiving Day*	2nd ♉ **27**	2nd ♉ **28** ♆ D 7:36 pm	
3	**4**	**5**	
10	**11**	**12**	

ASPECTS & MOON PHASES

☌ Conjunction	0°	● New Moon	(1st Quarter)
⚹ Sextile	60°	◐ Waxing Moon	(2nd Quarter)
□ Square	90°	○ Full Moon	(3rd Quarter)
△ Trine	120°	◑ Waning Moon	(4th Quarter)
⚻ Quincunx	150°		
☍ Opposition	180°		

DECEMBER 2020

SU	M	T	W
29	30	1 ♂️ 3rd ♊ ☿ → ♐ 2:51 pm ☽ → ♋ 10:33 pm	2 3rd ♋
6 3rd ♌ ☽ → ♍ 2:46 pm	7 ◑ 3rd ♍ 4th Quarter 7:37 pm	8 4th ♍ ☽ v/c 5:35 pm ☽ → ♎ 7:01 pm	9 4th ♎
13 4th ♐	14 ● 4th ♐ ☽ v/c 11:17 am New Moon 11:17 am ☽ → ♑ 10:35 pm *New Moon* *Solar Eclipse*	15 1st ♑ ♀ → ♐ 11:21 am	16 1st ♑
20 1st ♓ ☿ → ♑ 6:07 pm	21 ◐ 1st ♓ ☉ → ♑ 5:02 am ☽ v/c 5:25 am ☽ → ♈ 5:32 pm 2nd Quarter 6:41 pm *Yule* *Sun enters Capricorn* *Winter Solstice*	22 2nd ♈	23 2nd ♈ ☽ v/c 5:51 pm
27 2nd ♊	28 2nd ♊ ☽ v/c 10:01 pm	29 ○ 2nd ♊ ☽ → ♋ 5:28 am Full Moon 10:28 pm *Long Nights Moon*	30 3rd ♋
3	4	5	6

Eastern Standard Time (EST)

ZODIAC SIGNS

♈ Aries	♌ Leo	♐ Sagittarius
♉ Taurus	♍ Virgo	♑ Capricorn
♊ Gemini	♎ Libra	♒ Aquarius
♋ Cancer	♏ Scorpio	♓ Pisces

PLANETS

☉ Sun	♃ Jupiter
☽ Moon	♄ Saturn
☿ Mercury	♅ Uranus
♀ Venus	♆ Neptune
♂ Mars	♇ Pluto

DECEMBER 2020

TH	F	SA	NOTES
3 3rd ♋	**4** 3rd ♋ ☽ v/c 5:29 am ☽ → ♌ 7:53 am	**5** 3rd ♌ ☽ v/c 5:28 pm	
10 4th ♎ ☽ v/c 7:56 pm ☽ → ♏ 8:59 pm	**11** 4th ♏	**12** 4th ♏ ☽ v/c 8:58 pm ☽ → ♐ 9:39 pm	
17 1st ♑ ♄ → ♒ 12:04 am ☽ v/c 12:34 am ☽ → ♒ 1:27 am	**18** 1st ♒	**19** 1st ♒ ☽ v/c 3:45 am ☽ → ♓ 7:39 am ♃ → ♒ 8:07 am	
24 2nd ♈ ☽ → ♉ 5:55 am Christmas Eve	**25** 2nd ♉ Christmas Day	**26** 2nd ♉ ☽ v/c 6:32 am ☽ → ♊ 6:33 pm	
31 3rd ♋ ☽ v/c 8:45 am ☽ → ♌ 1:58 pm New Year's Eve	*1*	*2*	
7	*8*	*9*	

Aspects & Moon Phases

☌ Conjunction	0°	● New Moon	(1st Quarter)
✶ Sextile	60°	◑ Waxing Moon	(2nd Quarter)
□ Square	90°	○ Full Moon	(3rd Quarter)
△ Trine	120°	◑ Waning Moon	(4th Quarter)
⊼ Quincunx	150°		
☍ Opposition	180°		

Llewellyn's 2020 Witches' Calendar

Since 1998, *Llewellyn's Witches' Calendar* has been a favorite way to mark the turning of the Wheel of the Year. This beautiful calendar features magical wisdom, astrological data, and Witch's holidays, making it the perfect choice for bringing more happiness and enchantment into your year.

Each month features beautiful, original art by award-winning illustrator Jennifer Hewitson as well as an inspiring article and spell or ritual.

978-0-7387-4951-8, 28 pp., 12 x 12 $14.99

To order, call 1-877-NEW-WRLD or visit llewellyn.com
Prices subject to change without notice

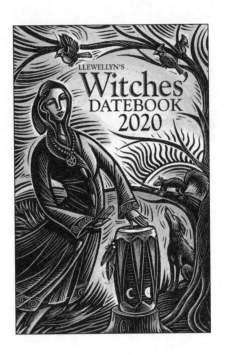

Llewellyn's 2020 Witches' Datebook

Live better, stay organized, and celebrate your Craft every day with *Llewellyn's 2020 Witches' Datebook*. This wonderful tool features beautiful illustrations from award-winning artist Jennifer Hewitson, a variety of ways to celebrate the Wheel of the Year, and powerful wisdom from practicing witches.

Find fresh ways to celebrate the sacred seasons and enhance your practice with sabbat musings (Barbara Moore), tasty sabbat recipes (Anna Franklin), witchy tips (Elizabeth Barrette), and essential oils (Tess Whitehurst). Also included are fascinating articles on guiding goddess archetypes (Danielle Blackwood), pop-culture protection magick (Emily Carlin), chakra healing (Melissa Tipton), honoring personally sacred days (Laura Tempest Zakroff), and more. This indispensable, on-the-go tool will make all your days more magical.

978-0-7387-4953-2, 168 pp., 5¼ x 8 $12.99

To order, call 1-877-NEW-WRLD or visit llewellyn.com

Prices subject to change without notice

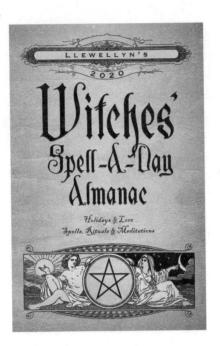

Llewellyn's
2020
Witches'
Spell-A-Day
Almanac

Holidays & Lore
Spells, Rituals & Meditations

Llewellyn's 2020 Witches' Spell–A–Day Almanac

Enjoy a new spell every day with *Llewellyn's 2020 Witches' Spell-A-Day Almanac*. Spellcasters of all levels can enhance their daily life with these easy bewitchments, recipes, rituals, and meditations. These 365 spells—supplied by popular magic practitioners like Tess Whitehurst, Raven Digitalis, Thuri Calafia, Melissa Tipton, Kate Freuler, Susan Pesznecker, and Jason and Ari Mankey—require minimal supplies and are helpful for every occasion.

For convenience, the 365 spells are cross-referenced by purpose, including love, health, money, protection, home and garden, travel, and communication. Discover beginner-friendly advice on the best time, place, and tools for performing each spell. Apply daily color and incense recommendations and astrological data to enhance each day's magic. And with space to jot down notes, this unique spell book can be used as a Book of Shadows.

978-0-7387-4954-9, 264 pp., 5¼ x 8 $12.99

To order, call 1-877-NEW-WRLD or visit llewellyn.com
Prices subject to change without notice

GET MORE AT LLEWELLYN.COM

Visit us online to browse hundreds of our books and decks, plus sign up to receive our e-newsletters and exclusive online offers.

- Free tarot readings • Spell-a-Day • Moon phases
- Recipes, spells, and tips • Blogs • Encyclopedia
- Author interviews, articles, and upcoming events

GET SOCIAL WITH LLEWELLYN

Find us on  🐦 @LlewellynBooks

www.Facebook.com/LlewellynBooks

GET BOOKS AT LLEWELLYN

LLEWELLYN ORDERING INFORMATION

Order online: Visit our website at www.llewellyn.com to select your books and place an order on our secure server.

Order by phone:
- Call toll free within the US at 1-877-NEW-WRLD (1-877-639-9753)
- We accept VISA, MasterCard, American Express, and Discover.
- Canadian customers must use credit cards.

Order by mail:
Send the full price of your order (MN residents add 6.875% sales tax) in US funds plus postage and handling to: Llewellyn Worldwide, 2143 Wooddale Drive, Woodbury, MN 55125-2989

POSTAGE AND HANDLING

STANDARD (US):
(Please allow 12 business days)
$30.00 and under, add $6.00.
$30.01 and over, FREE SHIPPING.

INTERNATIONAL ORDERS,
INCLUDING CANADA:
$16.00 for one book, plus $3.00 for each additional book.

Visit us online for more shipping options.
Prices subject to change.